MAKE YOUR OWN
KITCHEN TOOLS

SIMPLE WOODWORKING PROJECTS *for* EVERYDAY USE

MAKE YOUR OWN
KITCHEN TOOLS

SIMPLE WOODWORKING PROJECTS *for* EVERYDAY USE

DAVID PICCIUTO

Text © 2020 by Cedar Lane Press
Step-by-step photographs © 2020 by Daniel Struffolino
Cover and chapter opener photographs © 2020 by Danielle Atkins

All rights reserved. Excepting patterns, no part of this book may be reproduced or transmitted in any form or by any means, electric or mechanical, including photocopying, recording, or by any information storage and retrieval system, without written permission from the Publisher. Readers may make copies of patterns for personal use. The patterns themselves, however, are not to be duplicated for resale or distribution under any circumstances. Any such copying is a violation of copyright law.

Publisher: Paul McGahren
Editor: Kerri Grzybicki
Designer: Lindsay Hess
Layout Designer and Illustrator: Jodie Delohery
Step-by-Step Photographer: Daniel Struffolino

Cedar Lane Press
PO Box 5424
Lancaster, PA 17606-5424

Paperback ISBN: 978-1-950934-02-7
ePub ISBN: 978-1-950934-05-8
Library of Congress Control Number: 2020946269

Printed in the United States of America
10 9 8 7 6 5 4 3 2 1

Note: The following list contains names used in *Make Your Own Kitchen Tools* that may be registered with the United States Copyright Office: 3M; Apple iPad; BESSEY; Everbilt; Festool; Gardena; Gorilla Glue; HexArmor Rig Lizard; KenCraft Company; King Arthur's Tools; Kreg; Odie's Oil; MICROJIG; SawStop; Sharpie; Titebond; YouTube; Zhen.

Thank you to Kencraft Hardwoods for supplying materials used in this book. Visit https://www.kencraftcompany.com.

The information in this book is given in good faith; however, no warranty is given, nor are results guaranteed. Woodworking is inherently dangerous. Your safety is your responsibility. Neither Cedar Lane Press nor the author assume any responsibility for any injuries or accidents.

To learn more about Cedar Lane Press books, or to find a retailer near you, email info@cedarlanepress.com or visit us at www.cedarlanepress.com.

CONTENTS

INTRODUCTION | page 7

PIZZA ROCKER
page 8

BEER CADDY
page 20

SCOOP
page 28

BREAD SLICER
page 36

RUSTIC BOWL
page 46

EGG TRAY
page 54

KNIFE HANDLE
page 60

SEGMENTED BOWL
page 66

SERVING TRAY
page 78

SPOON & SPATULA
page 94

TRIVET
page 102

UTENSIL HOLDER
page 110

SPICE RACK
page 122

PIZZA PEEL
page 136

TABLET HOLDER
page 148

CHOOSING & USING FOOD-SAFE FINISHES
page 158

TOOLS YOU WILL NEED
page 162

METRIC CONVERSIONS
page 163

INDEX
page 164

MAKE YOUR OWN KITCHEN TOOLS

INTRODUCTION

Aside from our love of woodworking, one thing we woodworkers all have in common is food. We all have to eat. In fact, some of us even like to cook. If you think about it, cooking and woodworking are one and the same: a project comes to mind, and then you pull together the materials, gather the tools, and immerse yourself in the process. I guess the only difference with cooking is you get to eat your project—and enjoy a libation or two while putting it together.

This mindset fueled my previous book, *Make Your Own Cutting Boards*. A cutting board is an immensely popular project because every kitchen needs one. It's often a beginner's first woodworking project. For the seasoned woodworker, it's the perfect go-to handmade gift. What I've since realized is how many other woodworking projects a busy kitchen needs—and how many I've built during my time in the workshop.

With that in mind, I thought sharing these kitchen tools might be an interesting idea. The projects you'll find in this book range from simple, requiring only limited tools and time, to a few less-simple options that might need a deeper toolbox. Most important, I wanted to share projects—like the pizza rocker, segmented bowl, and knife handle—that involve techniques you might have considered complicated, but are actually a lot easier than you thought. In the end, regardless of your skill level or the square footage of your shop, I hope these projects provide the how-to and inspiration to make some long-lasting gear that you'll proudly put to work in your kitchen or happily give away as a gift. I believe everyone has the ability to be creative if they search for it within themselves—or simply listen to the rumbling call of hunger. Let's head to the woodshop and get cooking!

David Picciuto
Make Something

Website—www.MakeSomething.com
YouTube—www.youtube.com/MakeSomething
Twitter—www.twitter.com/drunkenwood
Facebook—www.facebook.com/MakeSomethingTV
Instagram—www.instagram.com/MakeSomethingTV

KITCHEN TOOL
PIZZA ROCKER

Your handmade pie deserves more than a generic roller.

TOOLS
- Permanent marker
- Ruler
- Jigsaw with metal-cutting blade
- Belt sander with 80-grit sandpaper
- Hand, eye, and lung protection
- Random orbital sander
- Tablesaw and push stick
- Bandsaw
- Router with 1/8" roundover bit
- Clamps
- Five-minute epoxy
- Drill with 1/4" wood bit
- Hacksaw
- Mallet
- Food-safe finish

MATERIALS
- 20-ga. stainless steel sheet, 5" x 15"
- 1/4"-diameter brass dowel
- Handle, hardwood*, 3/4" x 2 1/2" x 15 1/4"

* Throughout this book, when I refer to "hardwood," I mean domestic hardwood. Use walnut, oak, cherry, birch, maple, or whatever species you prefer.

Homemade pizza is a mainstay at my house, but I never knew how much fun cutting up a freshly cooked pie could be until I made a rocker. This baby doesn't fool around; the hefty blade cleanly slices the thickest of crusts and layers of toppings. After three or four stylish passes, your slice of bubbling hot pizza slides free without dragging that annoying extra cheese or its unsuspecting neighbor. This project also makes an excellent gift for your pizza-loving friends.

PLAN

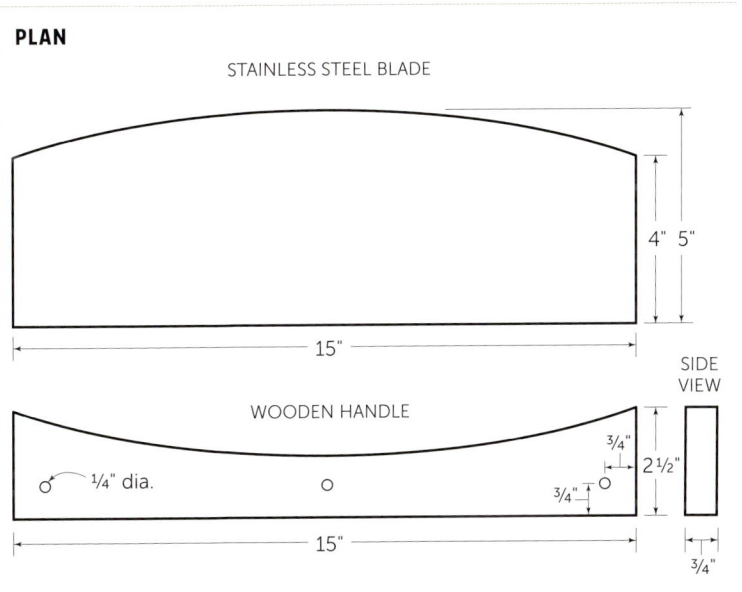

MAKE YOUR OWN KITCHEN TOOLS

PIZZA ROCKER

— 1 —

Start by drawing. Mark a 4" x 15" rectangle on your stainless steel. Draw a second line at 5" and mark the center at 7 ½" to indicate the crest of the curve. Freehand a rounded edge from the center of the crest to the 4" marks. You can also use a cardboard template and trace it.

— 2 —

Cut out the steel shape. Make sure to use a new metal cutting blade on your jigsaw, take your time, and take breaks to allow the blade to cool. Cut as close to the line as possible without touching it.

PIZZA ROCKER

— 3 —

Clean it up. Smooth the edges of the cutting blade down to the line with 80-grit sandpaper on a belt sander or a disc sander. (Sheets of sandpaper on a flat surface also work if you've got the elbow grease.) Be sure to wear hand, eye, and lung protection when sanding steel.

— 4 —

Mark the cutting bevel. Use a permanent marker to draw a line that matches the rounded edge about 3/16" in.

MAKE YOUR OWN KITCHEN TOOLS

PIZZA ROCKER

— 5 —

Sand the bevel. Angle the blade and use a belt sander (or sandpaper and block) to sand the bevel on each side to the 3/16" marker line.

— 6 —

Make it shine. Sand the faces of the blade to your desired sheen. The higher grit you go, the more mirrorlike the finish.

PIZZA ROCKER

— 7 —

Begin the handle. Cut a piece of hardwood to ¾" x 2½" x 15¼". This is cut slightly longer so it can be sanded down to the finished size.

— 8 —

Create a decorative look. To give your pizza rocker a better look, draw a curved line instead of a straight line on the wood where the handle will meet the blade. Use the curvature of the blade as your template.

MAKE YOUR OWN KITCHEN TOOLS

PIZZA ROCKER

— 9 —

Cut along the curved line. Use a bandsaw or jigsaw to cut along the curved line you just drew. Follow that up by sanding the curve smooth.

— 10 —

Cut the handle in half down the middle. With it cut to a curve and sanded smooth, resaw the handle right down the middle to make up the two halves that will sandwich the cutting blade.

— 11 —

Give the curved edge a roundover. Add a small ⅛" roundover on the outside face of each piece. Do not round over the inside that will make contact with the blade. This roundover is easier to do before assembly.

— 12 —

Glue it up. Use five-minute epoxy to glue the blade between the two handle halves. Clamp it together and allow to dry for 24 hours.

PIZZA ROCKER

— 13 —

Mark the holes. With the glue dried, mark the holes to be used for the brass dowels. Mark a horizontal line ¾" in from the top and the two outside dowels inset ¾" from the edge. Put the third hole directly in the center.

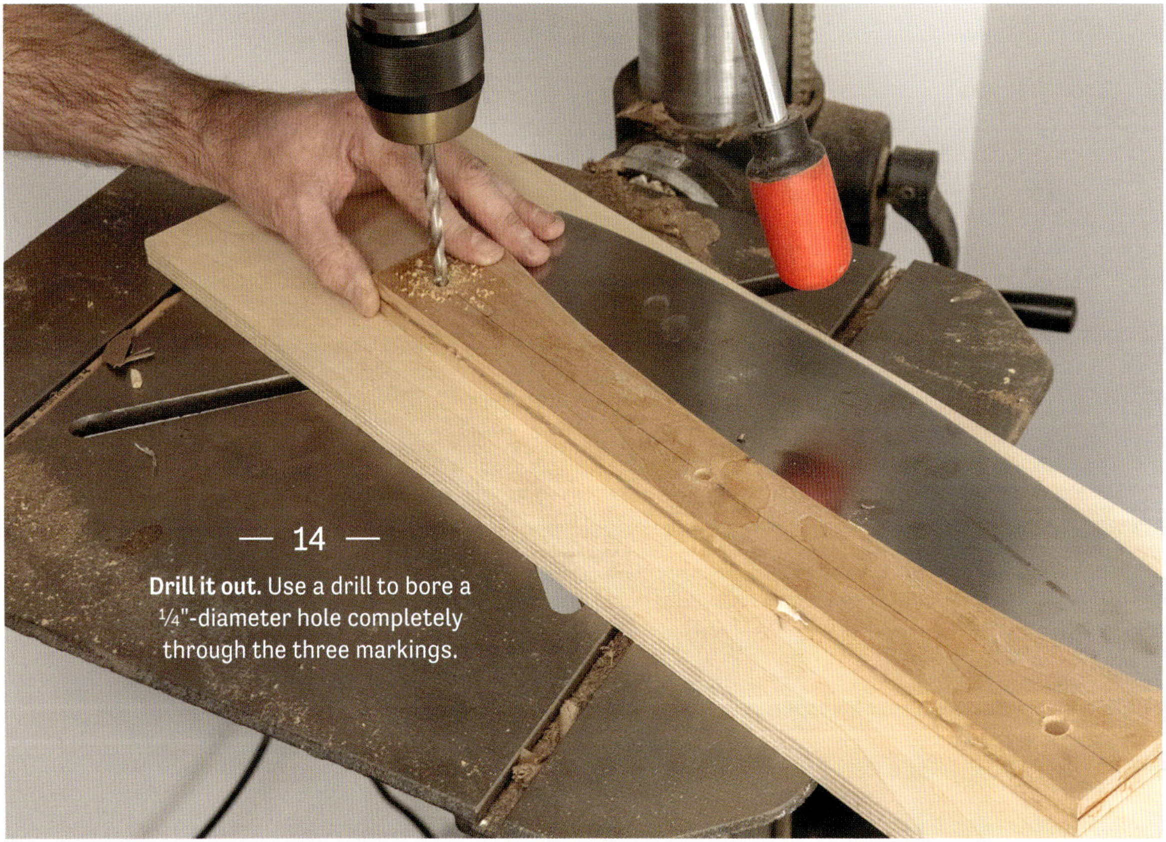

— 14 —

Drill it out. Use a drill to bore a ¼"-diameter hole completely through the three markings.

PIZZA ROCKER

— 15 —

Cut the brass dowels. Using a hacksaw, cut some ¼"-diameter brass rod slightly longer than the thickness of your assembled handle.

— 16 —

Add the brass dowels. Apply some epoxy to secure them and pound in the dowels.

MAKE YOUR OWN KITCHEN TOOLS

PIZZA ROCKER

— 17 —
Sand everything smooth. Once everything is dry, sand all handle edges so the steel and wood create a nice flush edge. Use the belt sander to flush the brass dowels as well.

— 18 —
Add rounded edges. Round over the outside edges of the handle so the cutter has a nice feel when using it. Use a 1/8" roundover bit like you did in Step 11.

PIZZA ROCKER

— 19 —

Give it one final sand. Do a few passes with your sander or sandpaper up to 220 grit.

— 20 —

Seal it up. Finish the hardwood handle with a food-safe oil. Any off-the-shelf cutting board oil will do the trick.

MAKE YOUR OWN KITCHEN TOOLS

KITCHEN TOOL
BEER CADDY

Transport your favorite brew in style.

TOOLS

- Tablesaw and push stick
- Pencil
- Ruler
- Drill with ⅝" Forstner drill bit and ¼" wood bit
- Bandsaw
- Disc sander
- Wood glue
- Clamps
- Flush-cut trim saw
- Finish

MATERIALS

- Hardwood, ½" x 7" x 31", cut into the following pieces:
  - (2) tall side pieces: 6½" x 11"
  - (2) long side pieces: 4" x 9"
  - (1) long divider: 9" x 3"
  - (2) short dividers: 5½" x 3"
- Bottom, plywood, ⅛" x 5¾" x 9"
- Handle, dowel, ⅝"-dia. x 10" long
- Reinforcement, dowel, ¼"-dia. x 6" long

If the area where you live is anything like mine, there is now a healthy crop of new and sustained local beer breweries around. They put so much thought into every handbrewed bottle of beer—why not craft a beer caddy to match? This six-pack holder will catch the eye of all discerning beer lovers.

TEMPLATE

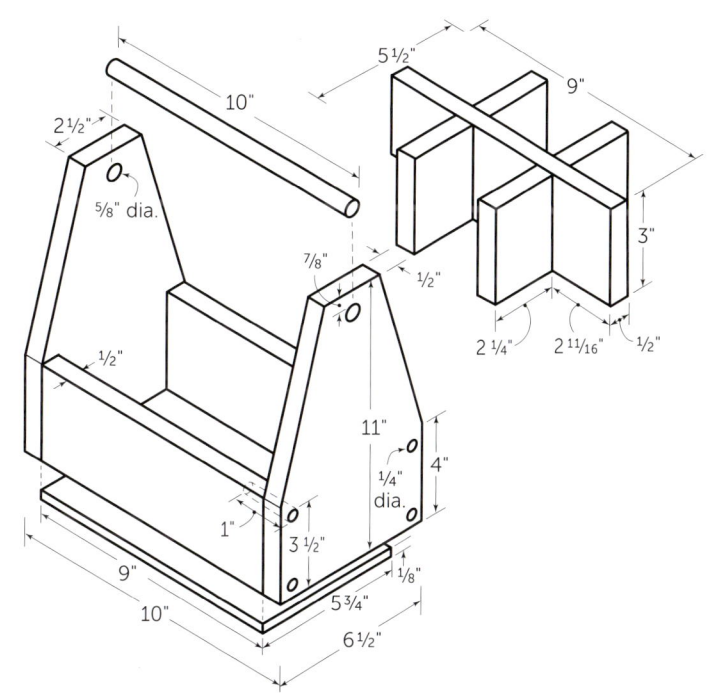

MAKE YOUR OWN KITCHEN TOOLS

BEER CADDY

— 1 —

Cut the hardwood pieces. The great thing about this project is it how fast it comes together. All the pieces can be cut to width and length from the ½"-thick material right away. I'm using mahogany, but ½" birch plywood also works great. Cut the sizes as shown on page 21.

— 2 —

One more cut from the plywood. With 7 pieces cut from your ½" material, you'll need to cut one more from your ⅛"-thick plywood measuring 5¾" x 9".

22 MAKE YOUR OWN KITCHEN TOOLS

BEER CADDY

— 3 —
Measure and mark your handle hole. Take both of the 6½" x 11" pieces, which will be the tall side panels, and place a mark ⅞" from the top and 3¼" from the edge for the handle.

— 4 —
Drill your handle holes. Drill a ⅝" hole with a handheld drill or drill press. For efficiency and accuracy, you can stack and drill both holes at the same time.

— 5 —
Taper the side panels. Mark your lines for the tapered side panels. From the top, make a mark 2" in from both sides. Make another mark on both sides 4" from the bottom and connect them to create the tapered lines.

MAKE YOUR OWN KITCHEN TOOLS   23

BEER CADDY

— 6 —

Cut the tapered side panels. Cut them to shape with a jigsaw or bandsaw. Cut close to the line but don't touch it so it can be cleaned up in the next step.

— 7 —

Smooth to the tapered line. Using a disc, palm, or orbit sander, sand down to the line to clean up the edges.

— 8 —

Cut the grooves for the bottom. On the two 4" x 9" long side pieces, cut a ⅛"-wide groove ³⁄₁₆" deep and about ¼" from the bottom (exact placement isn't critical) to hold the plywood bottom.

BEER CADDY

— 9 —

Measure your handle. Roughly assemble the pieces to determine the exact length to cut your dowel handle. It should be pretty close to 10". Cut it to length.

— 10 —

Assemble the caddy. Add glue to the dowel handle and on the end grain of the two long side pieces. Don't forget to add your plywood bottom! (I've done this). The plywood bottom does not need glue and can float in the grooves.

MAKE YOUR OWN KITCHEN TOOLS 25

BEER CADDY

— 11 —

Strengthen the joints. Reinforce the butt joints with some ¼" dowels. Measure ¼" in from the sides. The two bottom holes are 1" from the bottom and the two upper holes are 3½" from the bottom. With a ¼" bit, drill about 1" deep, add some glue and pound in your ¼" dowel.

— 12 —

Clean up the dowels. Cut off the excess dowel with a flush-cut trim saw.

— 13 —

Use the last three pieces as a divider. On the two small pieces, you'll want to draw a ½"-wide notch directly in the center and halfway down. On the long piece, draw two ½" notches, evenly spaced. That space is 2 $\tfrac{11}{16}$", but don't worry about it being exact. There's room for play.

— 14 —

Assemble the six-pack divider. Cut out the notches with a bandsaw or jigsaw. The three pieces should fit together without needing any glue to hold them in place.

— 15 —

Finish it up! Apply your favorite finish and that's it. You've got a beer caddy ready to fill with your chosen libation.

KITCHEN TOOL
SCOOP

For coffee beans, flour, or whatever else needs scooping.

A tried-and-true piece of baking advice says never to scoop your flour with the measuring cup—you'll compact the flour, including more in your recipe than desired. Avoid this by spooning flour out of your storage container with a handy scoop first and then leveling off the top of the cup. With how quickly and easily you can create these scoops, you can craft a whole fleet to manage whatever scoopables are in your kitchen.

TOOLS

- Wood glue
- Clamps
- Bandsaw with 3/16" 4 TPI skiptooth blade
- Pencil
- Round item for tracing curves
- Spindle sander
- Random orbital sander
- Toothpick
- Finish

MATERIALS

- Hardwood, 2¾" x 2¾" x 4½", or smaller pieces glued up

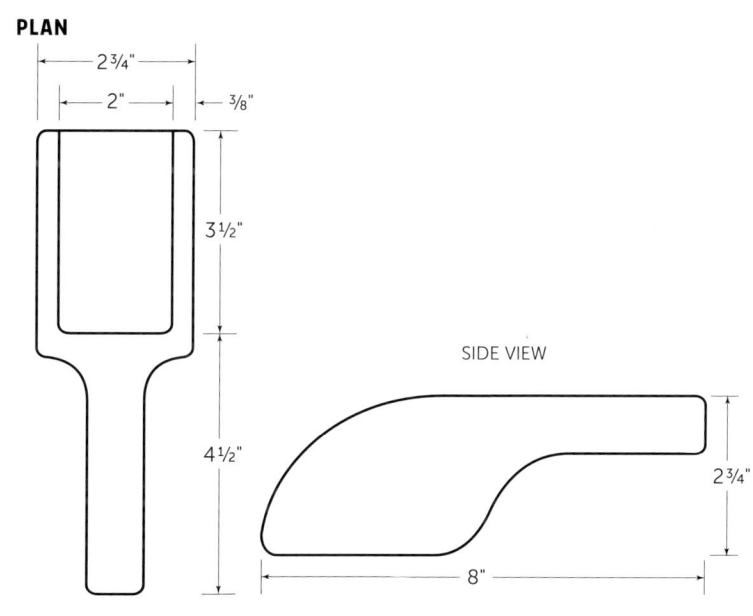

PLAN

SIDE VIEW

MAKE YOUR OWN KITCHEN TOOLS

SCOOP

— 1 —

Prepare the hardwood. You will need hardwood that is at least 2¾" thick for this project. Depending on your source, you may need to glue multiple boards together to achieve this. In this photo I have enough material to make two scoops.

— 2 —

Cut it to size. On a bandsaw, cut down your blank to the final dimensions of 2¾" x 2¾" x 4½". Don't worry about the rough surface left by the blade. Everything will be sanded and shaped later.

— 3 —

Draw the scoop lines. On one end of the blank, draw a U that offsets the outside edges by ⅜". Use a coin to round over the corners.

SCOOP

— 4 —

Cut out the scoop. Cut out the drawn curved line using a 3/16" 4 TPI skip tooth blade. This inside piece will be used as the handle, so make the cut in one continuous motion.

— 5 —

Apply glue to the inside cutout. The inside cutout from the blank will become the handle of the scoop. To attach it, add glue to one end.

MAKE YOUR OWN KITCHEN TOOLS   31

SCOOP

— 6 —

Glue it together. Glue the handle to the outside piece, overlapping about 1", and clamp it together. Don't worry if there are gaps. They will be filled later. Make sure to wipe away glue squeeze-out inside the scoop with a damp rag.

— 7 —

Draw the handle shape. Once the glue dries, freehand-draw the handle shape on the bottom of your scoop.

— 8 —

Cut out the handle. Using the same blade as before, cut out the handle on the bandsaw.

SCOOP

— 9 —

Design the profile. Draw the handle profile on the side of the scoop.

— 10 —

Carefully, cut the handle profile. NOTE: It is very important to start this cut with the handle tilted down on the table as seen here. If you enter this cut with the handle up off the table, the bandsaw blade will grab the piece and throw it down, potentially ruining the piece or even causing injury.

MAKE YOUR OWN KITCHEN TOOLS   33

SCOOP

— 11 —

Smooth out the handle. This can be done with files, rasps, and drill attachments, but I prefer the spindle sander and disc sander to round over and smooth out all the edges.

— 12 —

Finish the scoop design. With the handle shaped to your liking, draw the scoop profile.

— 13 —

One last cut. Make one final trip to the bandsaw to cut out the front of the scoop.

SCOOP

— 14 —

Sand it all down. Do a final shaping and sanding with a palm or a random orbital sander. Sand everything smooth to the touch so it feels good in your hand.

— 15 —

Fill any gaps. Any gaps left over from the glue up can be filled with a mixture of sawdust and wood glue. For a color match, make sure to use sawdust from the same species of wood used in the scoop.

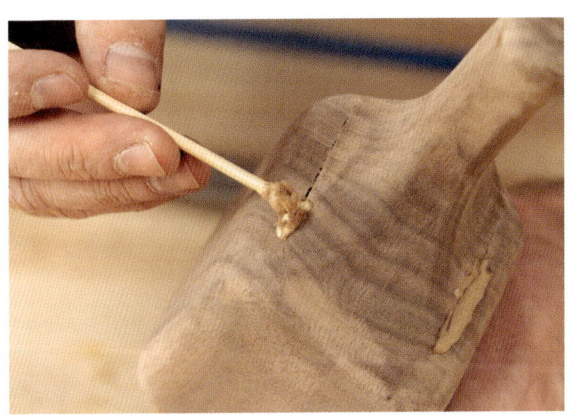

— 16 —

Apply your favorite finish. If your scoops will be used for food, use a cutting board wax or make your own with mixture of paraffin wax and mineral oil.

KITCHEN TOOL
BREAD SLICER

Fancy bread deserves a fancy slicer.

TOOLS

- Pencil
- Ruler
- Tablesaw
- Bandsaw
- Jointer
- Chopsaw
- Router with ½" roundover bit
- Compass
- Wood glue
- Clamps
- Painter's tape
- Sliding T-bevel
- Random orbital sander
- Food-safe finish

MATERIALS

- Hardwood, 2" x 4¾" x 24"

This handsome bread slicer makes it simple to cut a long, crisp-crusted French loaf into evenly sized pieces with a perfect bias. If you like extra-thick slices, just skip every other cutting slot. Partner one of these slicers with a few jars of local jam, honey, or butter for a thoughtful hostess gift.

PLAN

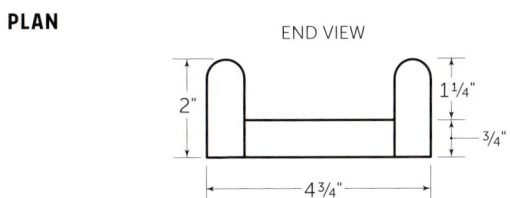

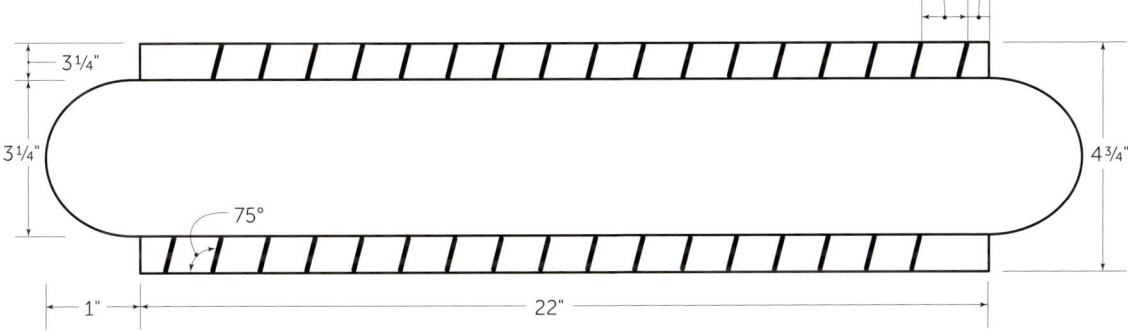

MAKE YOUR OWN KITCHEN TOOLS

BREAD SLICER

— 1 —
Start with a solid piece of wood. This solid piece measures 2" x 4¾" x 24". While you can use three separate pieces to make this project, I prefer a solid piece because when it's glued back together, the grain will line up. I've marked lines ¾" in from the sides and the bottom.

— 2 —
Make first cuts on the tablesaw. Rip the two ¾" sides off the blank.

BREAD SLICER

— 3 —

Cut the bottom. Resaw the ¾" bottom off the blank on the bandsaw.

— 4 —

Flatten the board. The bandsaw blade will leave a rough edge. Flatten that face using either a jointer, planer, or sander.

BREAD SLICER

— 5 —

The slicer starts to take shape. Here are the three pieces cut and sanded from the starting solid piece.

— 6 —

Determine the length. Measure 2" in from each end of the two long pieces and make a mark. In this photo I'm using a French baguette as a reference and a little motivation!

— 7 —

Cut the sides. Take the two long sides and cut off 2" from each end. As shown, you can cut both pieces at the same time.

— 8 —

Smooth the edges. Round over what will be the inside of both long sides with a ½" roundover bit at the router table.

— 9 —

Shape the bottom piece. With a compass or anything round, like a spray paint can, draw a half-circle on each end of the bottom piece.

BREAD SLICER

— 10 —

Round the ends. Cut the half circles at the bandsaw.

— 11 —

Put it all together. Glue the three pieces together with wood glue and a few clamps. The blue masking tape in this photo helps to align the pieces.

BREAD SLICER

— 12 —

Create your slicing angle. Use your sliding T-bevel and set it to 75°. The angle isn't critical, so anything close will work.

— 13 —

Make your angle marks. With your T-bevel, make your first mark ½" in from the edge. Make 16 more marks 1" apart, for a total of 17.

MAKE YOUR OWN KITCHEN TOOLS

BREAD SLICER

— 14 —

Cut the angled slots. Set your tablesaw miter fence to that same 75° angle using your sliding T-bevel and cross-cut the 17 slots. The blade should be about 1¼" high so it just cuts into the surface of the bottom piece. This will allow you to slice through the bottom of the bread.

— 15 —

Round over the bottom. For a nice decorative look, round over the bottom with a ½" roundover router bit.

— 16 —

Smooth it up. For the final sanding, I like to sand everything up to 220 grit for a nice, smooth feel.

BREAD SLICER

— 17 —

Add a nice finish. For a finish, use a food-safe wax, mineral oil, or cutting board finish.

— 18 —

Take it for a test drive! Grab a nice crunchy loaf, a bread knife, some cheese or jam, and get slicing. Enjoy!

MAKE YOUR OWN KITCHEN TOOLS

KITCHEN TOOL
RUSTIC BOWL

The carved, freeform shape makes this project a true original.

TOOLS

› Chisel
› Mallet
› Permanent marker
› Ruler
› Bandsaw
› Angle grinder with 4" power carving disc
› Bent gouge
› Hand and eye protection
› Clamps
› Hand plane
› Food-safe finish

MATERIALS

› Solid piece of tree trunk, small enough for your bandsaw

If you've ever wanted to try your hand at carving a bowl, this is the project for you. Find a solid log that will fit in your bandsaw and give this a go. The exact dimensions of your bowl will vary based on the size and shape of the log you choose. However, I suggest positioning the bowl within the half-log as shown in the illustration so as to maximize the natural curves of the log in the bowl's rim.

TEMPLATE

The bowl should be positioned with its opening at the curved side of the log. You will need to customize exact layout based on the size of the log.

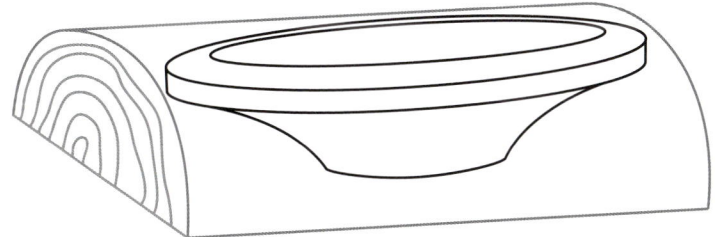

RUSTIC BOWL

— 1 —

Remove the bark using a chisel and mallet. Since I'm starting with a solid tree trunk, removing the bark is the first order of business. When choosing your wood, pick something small enough for your bandsaw to handle.

— 2 —

Mark the diameter. Draw a straight line right down the center of your blank.

48   MAKE YOUR OWN KITCHEN TOOLS

RUSTIC BOWL

— 3 —
Cut the blank in half. Be careful cutting the blank on the bandsaw. Keep your hands and body away from the exposed blade.

— 4 —
Create the shape of the bowl. Freehand-draw an oval on the curved side of the blank, leaving at least 1" on either side for a lip. Don't worry about it being a perfect oval. This project lends itself to organic shapes.

— 5 —
Break out some carving tools. You can use a variety of carving tools for this project, either hand tools or power carving. I used a mallet, a bent gouge, and a 4" power carving disc in an angle grinder.

MAKE YOUR OWN KITCHEN TOOLS   49

RUSTIC BOWL

— 6 —
Power carving will make the job easier. Mount the power carving disc on your angle grinder and carve away inside the line until you reach a desired depth and shape. Perfection is not necessary.

— 7 —
Any style works inside the bowl. Sand the inside smooth if you like or use a bent gouge and carve away decorative dimples that add character.

— 8 —
Draw an outside lip. Following the curve you just carved, freehand-draw the outside lip that will be the outside of the bowl. This outside lip offsets the inner curve by 1".

RUSTIC BOWL

— 9 —

Cut the outside line of the bowl. On your bandsaw, use a blade like the ³⁄₁₆" 4 TPI skiptooth blade. You want a low amount of teeth per inch so the blade can remove all the waste when cutting something this thick.

— 10 —

Carve the bottom of the bowl. Freehand-draw the bottom curves and start power carving. There will be a lot of material to remove, so take breaks and stay alert. Again, don't worry about the shape since a freeform organic feel is the goal. Be sure the piece is secure when you work with the grinder.

MAKE YOUR OWN KITCHEN TOOLS   51

RUSTIC BOWL

— 11 —

Flatten the bottom. A nice flat bottom is needed for the bowl to rest on. This can be accomplished with sanding or a hand plane.

— 12 —

Add some more character. Use the bent gouge to create a dimple texture along the outside.

— 13 —

Shape the lip of the bowl. Use your chisel and mallet to do some final shaping of the lip. Keep chiseling away until the shape and feel seem right.

RUSTIC BOWL

— 14 —

Apply a finish coat. For a dough bowl like this, food-safe wax, mineral oil, or cutting board finish is suggested.

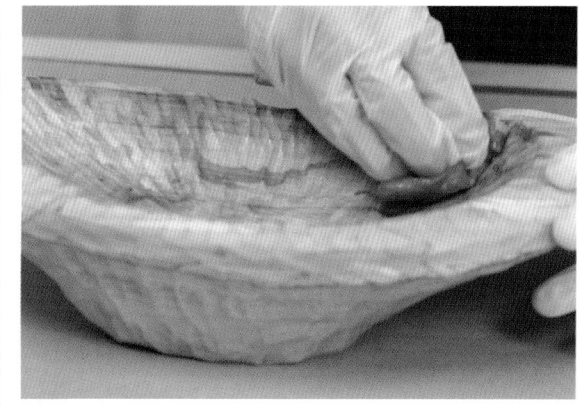

— 15 —

It's time to put your bowl to use! A fruit bowl, dough bowl, or maybe a centerpiece. It's all up to you. Enjoy!

KITCHEN TOOL
EGG TRAY

Keep those backyard-fresh eggs comfy in handcrafted style.

TOOLS

> Tablesaw and push stick
> Permanent marker
> Ruler
> Drill with 1½" Forstner bit
> Router with ⅛" roundover bit and 45° chamfer bit
> Bandsaw
> Wood glue
> Clamps
> Random orbital sander with sandpaper up to 220 grit
> Food-safe finish

MATERIALS

> Top, hardwood, ¾" x 4" x 12¼"
> Bottom, hardwood, ½" x 4" x 12¼"

Whether you prescribe to the European (non-washed and stored on the counter) or American (washed and kept refrigerated) egg storage rules for your backyard-fresh eggs,* this simple tray will hold them in style! The contrasting wood and corner bevels are eye-catching, yet easy to create.

*Note that if you do purchase your eggs from an American grocery, you will want to keep them in the fridge.

TEMPLATE

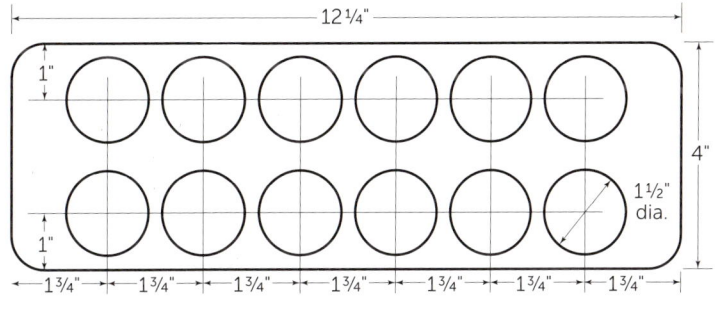

SIDE VIEW

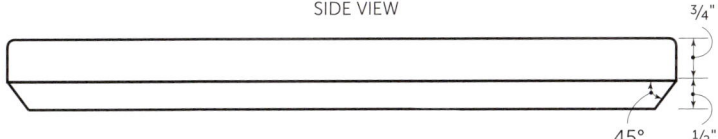

MAKE YOUR OWN KITCHEN TOOLS

EGG TRAY

— 1 —

Cut down the wood. Cut a piece of hardwood to measure ¾" x 4" x 12¼".

— 2 —

Mark the egg holes. Use the diagram on page 55 to mark the location of each hole.

EGG TRAY

— 3 —

Drill each of the holes. With a 1½" Forstner bit mounted in a drill press, drill all the way through the board. Make sure to have a sacrificial piece underneath to prevent blowout.

— 4 —

Smooth out the rough edges. Use a ⅛" roundover bit in the router table to round over the edges of all 12 holes.

— 5 —

Cut the bottom piece. On the bandsaw, cut a piece measuring ½" x 4" x 12¼" for the bottom. I'm using a piece of maple that contrasts nicely with the walnut for a decorative look.

MAKE YOUR OWN KITCHEN TOOLS

EGG TRAY

— 6 —

Glue and clamp the two pieces together. Be sure to not use too much glue. The squeeze-out is difficult to clean from the 12 drilled holes.

— 7 —

Lighten up the look of the tray. At this point, the tray is 1¼" thick. Use a chamfer bit along the bottom edges to lighten up the look. Always route the end grain first so if there's any tear out, it will be cleaned up when routing the long sides.

— 8 —

Smooth out the top of the tray. Use the ⅛" roundover bit to add a smooth curve to the top edges of the tray. If preferred, round corners also, or leave a little more squared off as shown in the photos.

EGG TRAY

— 9 —

Sand the surfaces. Use a random orbital sander or sanding method of choice to smooth the tray to 220 grit.

— 10 —

Apply your favorite finish. For this project, I'm using cutting board oil. It's easy to apply and refinish when needed.

MAKE YOUR OWN KITCHEN TOOLS

KITCHEN TOOL
KNIFE HANDLE

With its custom handmade handle, this knife will be your go-to blade.

TOOLS

- Painter's tape
- Bandsaw
- Pencil
- Drill with wood bit sized to fit rivets and a larger countersink bit if rivets have heads
- Hammer
- Sacrificial wood piece
- Spindle sander
- Random orbital sander with sandpaper up to 220 grit
- Steel wool up to #0000
- Finish

MATERIALS

- Knife kit of your choice
- Small piece of figured hardwood

Knife kits are a fantastic way to customize your kitchen, and the selection of blades is astounding. You can find knives in any style you can think of, and the metal used can be anything from normal carbon steel to 50+ layered Damascus steel. Take a look at your local woodworking store or online retailer to narrow down your choice. Because you only need a small piece of wood for the handle, it is an affordable project even if you use a highly figured hardwood.

TEMPLATE

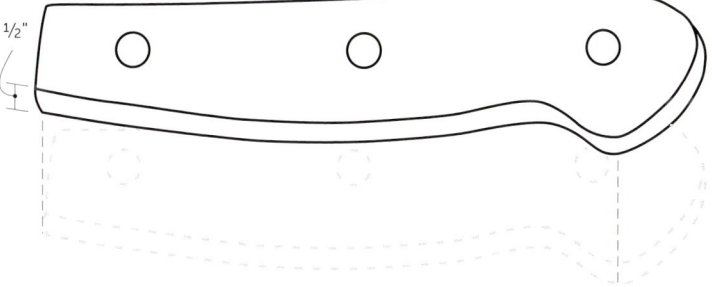

**Overall handle thickness and length, the placement of the rivets, and shape of handle will vary based on the knife kit selected.

MAKE YOUR OWN KITCHEN TOOLS

KNIFE HANDLE

— 1 —

Choose a knife kit. This project will work for any type of knife, but I chose a 7" chef's knife. You can find knife kits at your local woodworking retailers or online. For added safety while working with it, cover the sharp blade with some painter's tape.

— 2 —

Use wood that's thicker than the knife bolster. For its rich color and varied grain, I'm using ½"-thick figured koa. Trace the knife handle onto the wood. Flip the knife over and trace the other side onto the wood.

— 3 —

Cut the two handle shapes. With a bandsaw or jigsaw, cut just outside the line. It will get sanded down to the line later.

KNIFE HANDLE

— 4 —

Tape the two pieces together. Place your knife handle on top of the two pieces and trace out the holes for the rivets.

— 5 —

Drill out the rivet holes on the drill press. The size of the holes will depend on your kit. If you use a handheld drill, be sure to drill at a 90° angle.

KNIFE HANDLE

— 6 —

Drill a countersink if your rivets have a head. The rivets for this knife kit have a small head on them. As a result, I'm creating a countersink with a larger drill bit. This is not a necessary step if the rivets in your knife kit don't have a head.

— 7 —

Glue the wood pieces to the knife handle. Use a two-part epoxy to glue the wood to the handle and then pound in the rivets. Place a piece of metal or sacrificial wood under your knife when pounding in the rivets so they don't come through the other side and dent your bench.

— 8 —

Sand down the wood to the metal. If you don't have a spindle sander, you can purchase a sanding drum for your drill press.

KNIFE HANDLE

— 9 —

With the handle shaped, sand the faces flush. Start with 120 grit and work your way up to 220, being sure to smooth over the edges for a comfortable fit in your hand.

— 10 —

Create an extremely smooth finish. Use steel wool or non-woven sanding pads for an extremely smooth finish while polishing up the metal. Start with #00 and work your way up to #0000.

— 11 —

Finish it up. Apply a coat of oil to your beautiful knife. I used linseed oil.

MAKE YOUR OWN KITCHEN TOOLS

KITCHEN TOOL
SEGMENTED BOWL

Transform skinny stock into a full-sized bowl.

TOOLS

- Tablesaw with push stick and miter gauge fence
- Wood glue
- Painter's tape
- Belt sander
- Sandpaper
- Compass
- Bandsaw
- Clamps
- Drill with screwdriver bit
- Lathe with chuck
- Round carbide turning tool
- Handsaw
- Food-safe finish

Instead of starting with a chunk of wood, this project utilizes a creative gluing-up process to turn 16' of stock into a layered blank. From there, the turning process is quick; simply knock off the rings' corners and smooth the walls. Whether you have some stock to use up or just don't feel like hogging out a bowl interior from a chunk of wood, this project comes together in a quick and satisfying manner. You can use this same technique to create larger or smaller bowl sizes—imagine a salad set with a large bowl to toss and serve and a few individual bowls, or even a *hangiri* for mixing sushi rice.

MATERIALS

- Ring pieces, hardwood, from ¾" x 1" x 16' stock, cut to length:
  - (12) Top ring: 3 $\frac{1}{16}$"
  - (12) 2nd ring: 2 $\frac{7}{8}$"
  - (12) 3rd ring: 2 $\frac{11}{16}$"
  - (12) 4th ring: 2 ½"
  - (12) 5th ring: 2 $\frac{5}{16}$"
  - (12) Bottom ring: 2 $\frac{1}{8}$"
- Bottom, hardwood, ¾" x 7 ¼" dia.
- Screws

SEGMENTED BOWL

PLAN

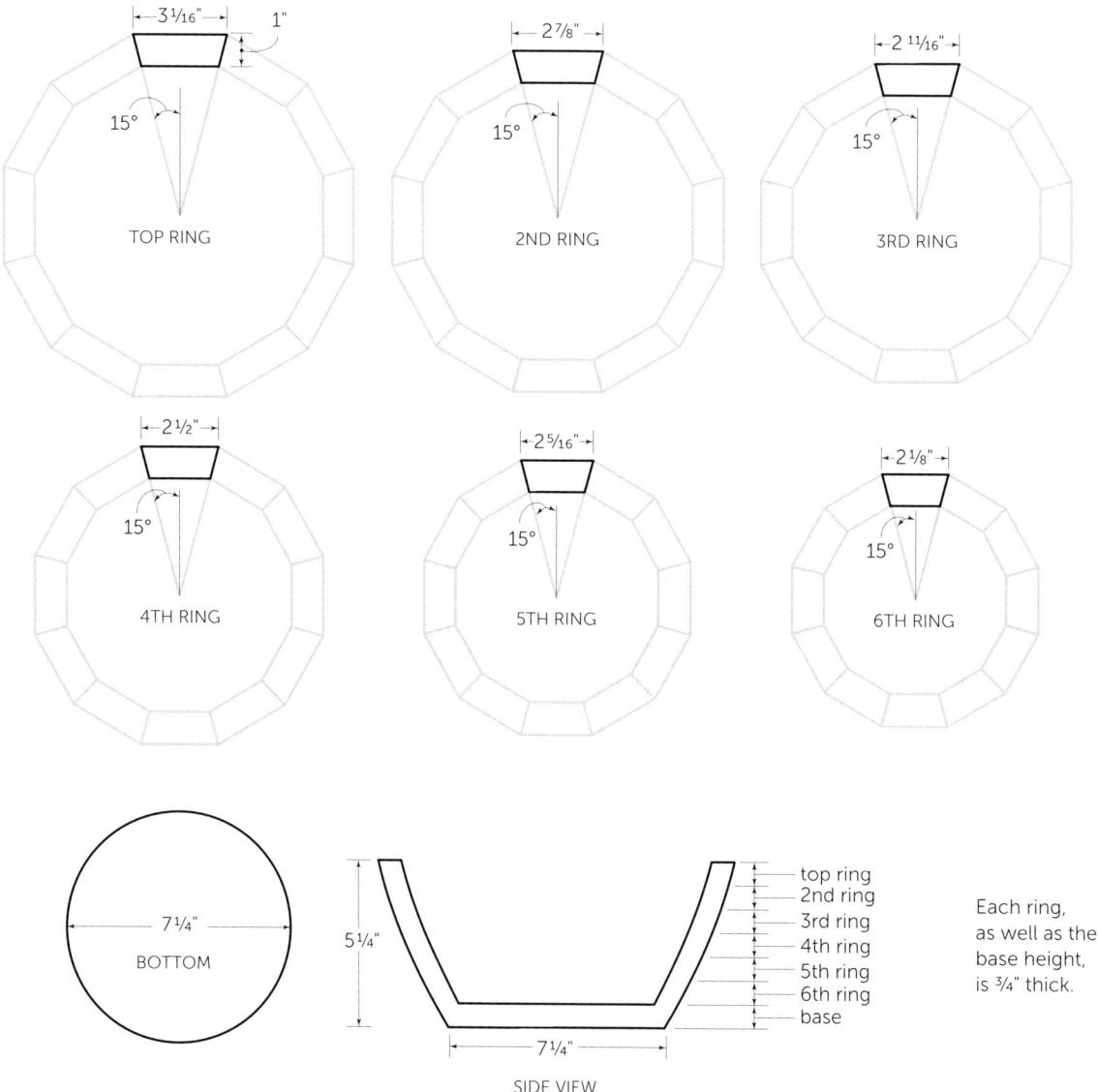

SEGMENTED BOWL

— 1 —

Rip the wood into 1"-wide strips. You'll need at least 16' of the 1"-wide strips to be ripped from the ¾" hardwood.

— 2 —

Set your saw at the correct angle. If cutting at the tablesaw, set your miter gauge fence to 15°. For a miter saw, set your blade to 15°.

— 3 —

Measure twice, cut once. Each ring of the bowl consists of 12 segments; measurements on page 67. Since the rings will decrease in diameter from top to bottom, the lengths of the segments will decrease as well. The length is measured on the longest side of the segment. If using a stop at the tablesaw, push your stock against the stop and lift up the stop before pushing through the blade. This will keep the small cutoffs from getting trapped between the blade and stop.

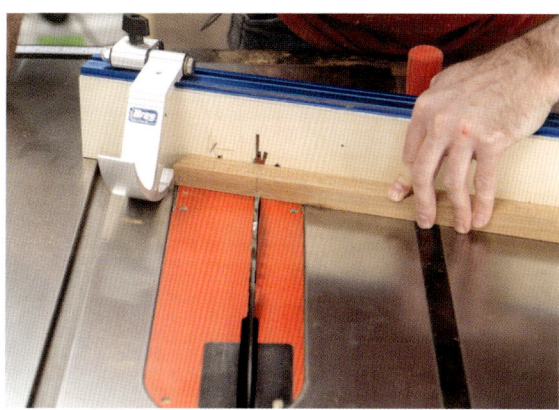

SEGMENTED BOWL

— 4 —

Start cutting the segments. Cut the 12 segments for the top ring at 3¹⁄₁₆" wide. Move your stop in for the next row and cut 12; and so on.

— 5 —

Apply the glue. Use painter's tape or masking tape as a clamp to glue half of each ring. Only gluing six segments together at a time will allow the correction of any errors in angle in step 7.

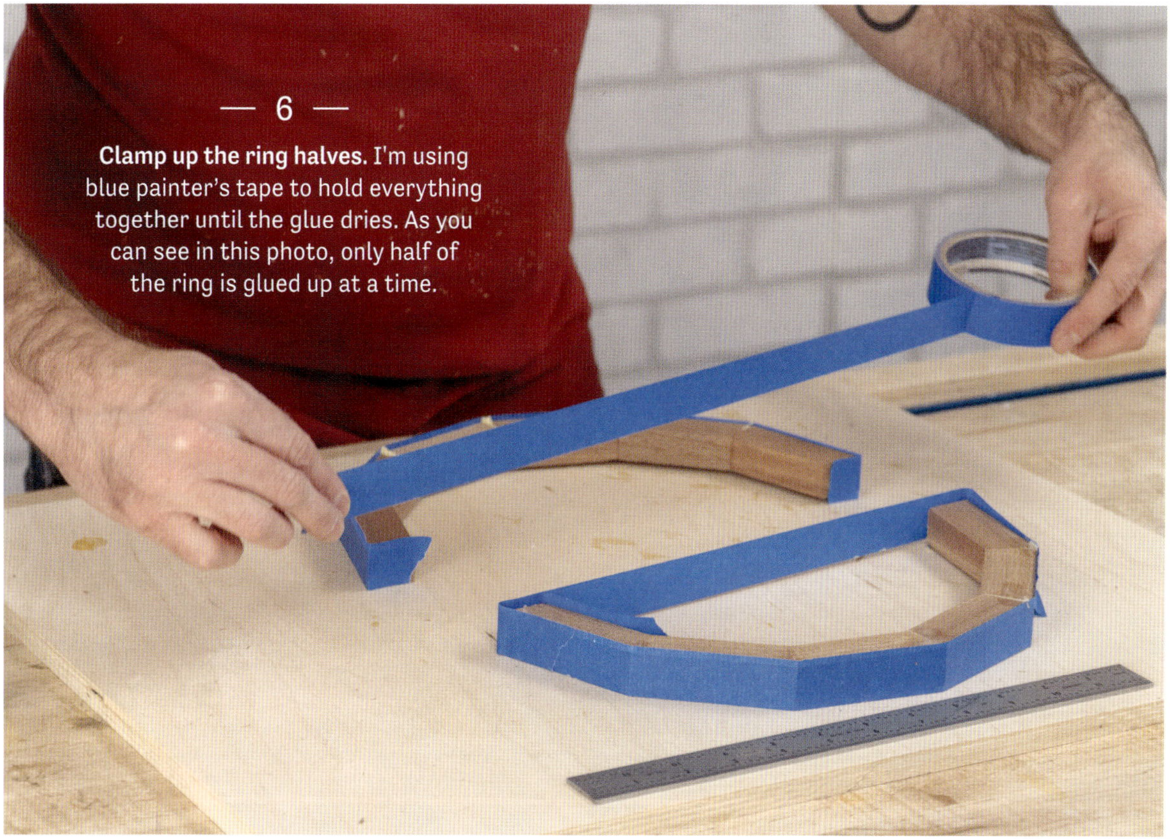

SEGMENTED BOWL

— 6 —

Clamp up the ring halves. I'm using blue painter's tape to hold everything together until the glue dries. As you can see in this photo, only half of the ring is glued up at a time.

— 7 —

Sand the edges. Once the glue dries, sand the edges so the faces are on the same plane to make up for any error in our angle. This can be done at a belt sander or by hand with sandpaper glued to a flat surface, like plywood.

MAKE YOUR OWN KITCHEN TOOLS   71

SEGMENTED BOWL

— 8 —

Glue the two halves together to complete the ring. Do this with all six rings.

— 9 —

Sand the top and bottom of each ring flat. Before gluing the rings together, you'll need them nice and smooth. This ensures a nice, tight glue-up. The photo shows adhesive-backed sandpaper on a piece of plywood.

— 10 —

Draw the bottom of the bowl. Draw a 7¼" circle on a solid piece of wood to create the bottom of the bowl.

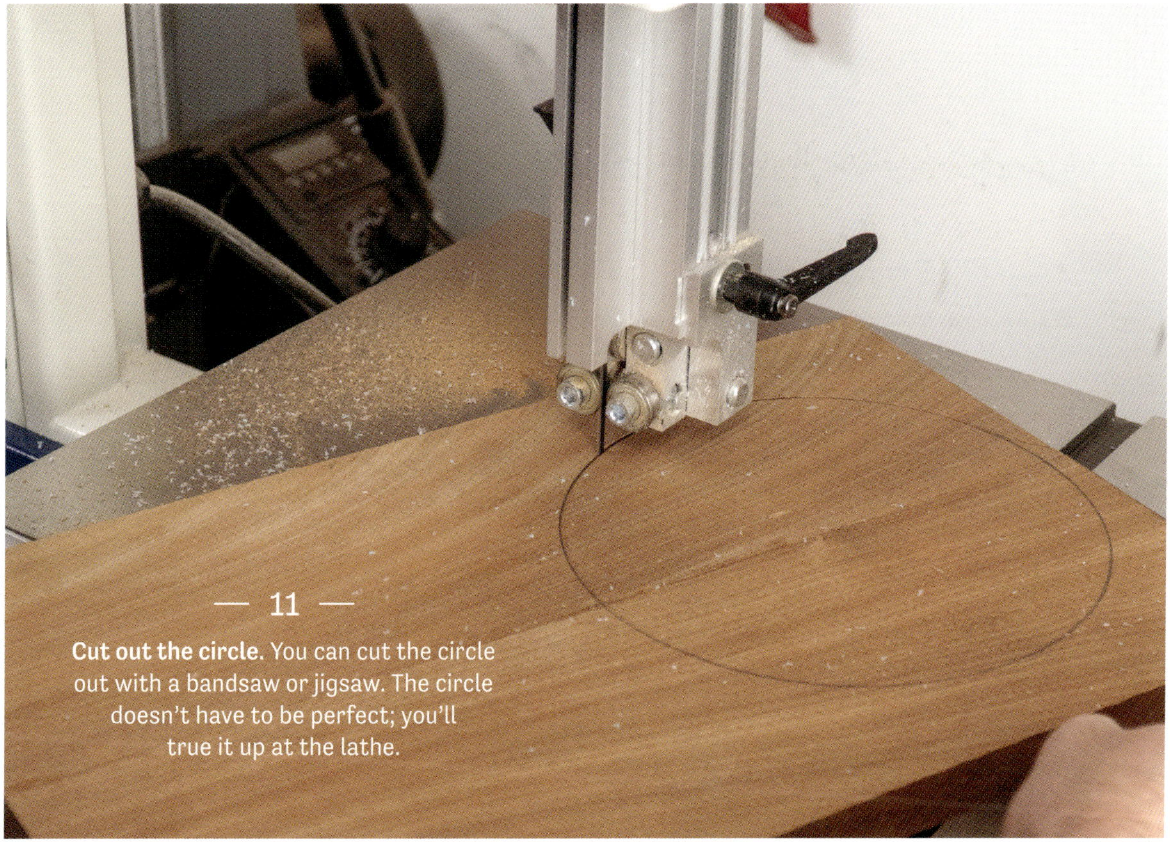

SEGMENTED BOWL

— 11 —
Cut out the circle. You can cut the circle out with a bandsaw or jigsaw. The circle doesn't have to be perfect; you'll true it up at the lathe.

— 12 —
Glue all the rings together. Add a 3½" plywood circle on the bottom (the top in this photo). That will be our sacrificial piece for chucking the bowl to the lathe.

SEGMENTED BOWL

— 13 —

Even out the pressure. This glue-up can be tricky, so adding a scrap piece of wood on top with a couple of clamps will even out the pressure.

— 14 —

Get it ready for the lathe. Let the glue dry for a couple of hours or more. Don't rush it. Once dry, screw your chuck to the bottom of the bowl and mount it on the lathe.

SEGMENTED BOWL

— 15 —

Start off with light passes. Use a light touch to start and continue until you get the outside shape smooth and to your desired shape.

— 16 —

Repeat the process for the inside of the bowl. I like using a round carbide turning tool for this process.

— 17 —

Sand everything smooth. Once you're done turning the bowl, sand everything smooth. This is much easier while the bowl is still chucked up in the lathe.

SEGMENTED BOWL

— 18 —

Remove the bowl from the lathe.
To remove the bowl, I like to carve away the sacrificial bottom, making sure I won't hit any screws. Leave about 1" of material to handcut the rest in the next step.

— 19 —

Cut the bowl from the sacrificial bottom.
With a handsaw and the lathe turned off, you can cut away your bowl from the bottom bottom.

SEGMENTED BOWL

— 20 —

Sand the bottom flat. Use a belt sander or sandpaper adhered to a flat surface.

— 21 —

Finish the hardwood with a food-safe oil. Any off-the-shelf cutting board oil will do.

MAKE YOUR OWN KITCHEN TOOLS

KITCHEN TOOL
SERVING TRAY

Carry ingredients and meals in style with this chic tray.

TOOLS

- Tablesaw and push stick
- Pencil and ruler
- Bandsaw with 3/16" 4 TPI skiptooth blade
- Random orbital sander
- Router with 1/4" roundover bit
- Wood glue
- Band clamp
- Spline jig
- Flush-cut trim saw
- Disc sander
- Drill with 1/2" and 1/4" wood bits
- Mallet
- Hacksaw
- Hex keys

You can use this handy tray to transport ingredients from kitchen to grill; convey condiments from fridge to table; or even carry a full-blown breakfast-in-bed to your favorite person. You can put the tray flat on the table or extend the legs to create a raised platform. Contrasting splines and cut-out handles lend an air of elegance to this useful kitchen tool.

MATERIALS

- 2 tray long sides, hardwood, 3/4" x 2" x 19 1/2"
- 2 tray short sides, hardwood, 3/4" x 2" x 11 1/2"
- Bottom, plywood, 1/8" x 10 3/4" x 18 3/4"
- 8 splines, contrasting hardwood, 1/8" x 1" x 2"
- 4 legs, hardwood, 3/4" x 3/4" x 8"
- 2 leg supports, dowels, 1/2" dia. x 10"
- Connecting bolts and cap nuts

SERVING TRAY

PLAN

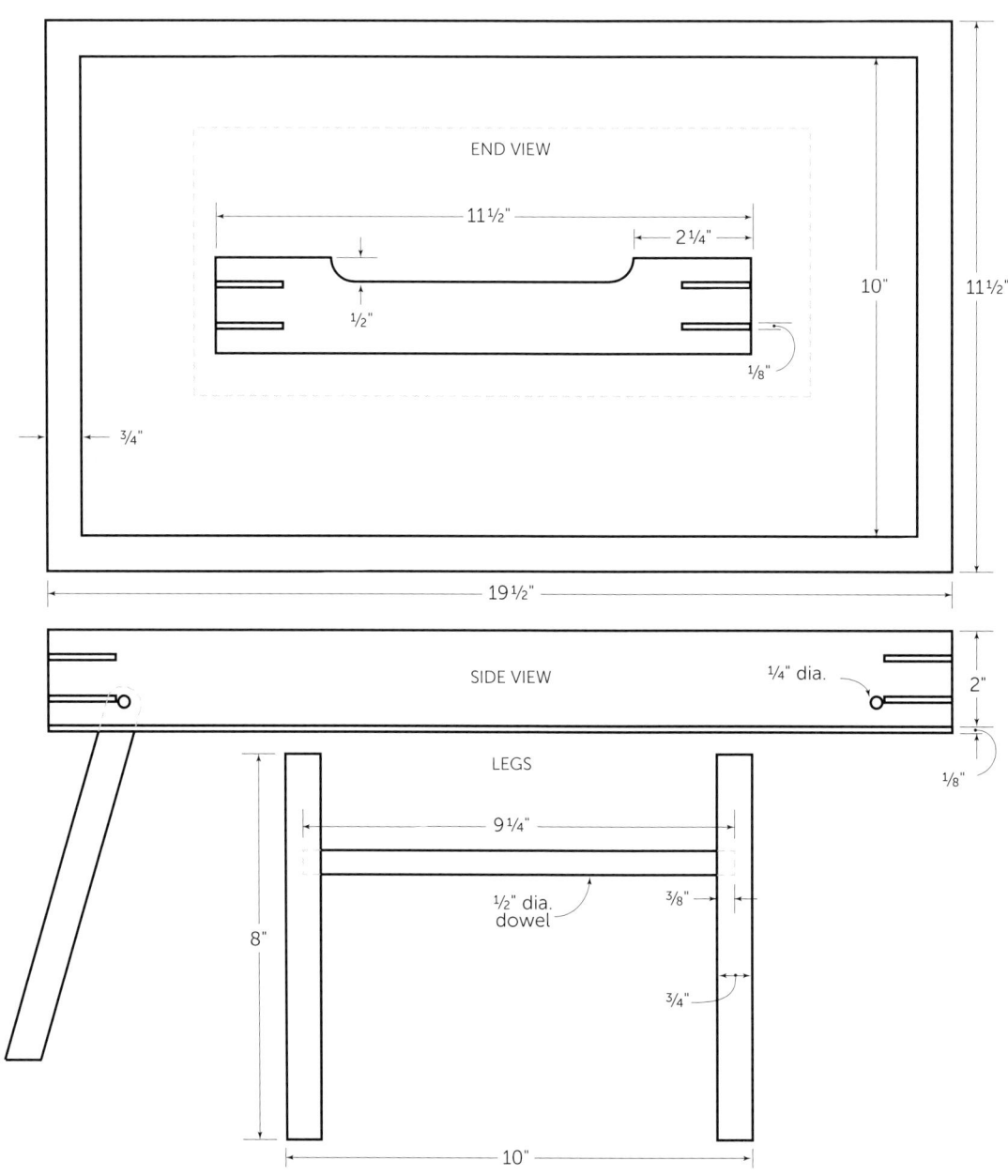

SERVING TRAY

— 1 —

Cut your materials to size. First thing you'll need to do is cut some ¾"-thick material into 2"-wide strips. You'll need two pieces at least 20" long and two pieces at least 12" long.

— 2 —

Cut the two long sides. Set your blade to 45° and cut two of the long sides to a length of 19½".

MAKE YOUR OWN KITCHEN TOOLS

SERVING TRAY

— 3 —

Cut the short sides. Cut the two short sides to a length of 11½". The angle of the cuts is the same setup as the long pieces.

— 4 —

Cut the grooves to hold the bottom. Return the tablesaw blade to 90° and set the height to ⅜". Cut a groove down the center along the inside of all four pieces. This groove will hold the ⅛"-thick plywood bottom.

SERVING TRAY

— 5 —
Check your work. The four pieces should look like this.

— 6 —
Cut the bottom out of ⅛"-thick plywood. The approximate size will be 10¾" x 18¾". It will be cut to fit so the four side pieces fit together during glue-up in step 11.

SERVING TRAY

— 7 —

Measure the handles. You'll cut material from the two short sides to form handles. Measure and mark 2¼" in from the sides and ½" in from the top to be cut away. Use a coin to draw in roundovers for the corners.

— 8 —

Cut out the handles. Cut out the material with a bandsaw. I'm using a ³⁄₁₆" 4 TPI skip tooth blade.

SERVING TRAY

— 9 —

Sand smooth. The bandsaw will likely leave a rough edge. Sand the cutaways smooth. You may need a spindle sander or round file for the curves.

— 10 —

Round the handles. Since these will be handles, I like to round them over with ¼" roundover bit at the router table to give them a nicer feel on the hands when carrying the tray.

— 11 —

Glue up the tray. Add some glue to the miters, place in the plywood bottom, and use a band clamp. Make sure the plywood bottom isn't so big that it interferes with the glue-up. Use masking tape if you don't have a band clamp.

MAKE YOUR OWN KITCHEN TOOLS

SERVING TRAY

— 12 —

Prepare a spline jig. Once the glue dries, we will reinforce the miters with splines. You can use a shop-made spline jig or purchase one from a woodworking supply store. (My video on how to do so can be found here: www.MakeSomething.com/splinejig)

— 13 —

Cut spline grooves. For the splines, I'm cutting two grooves about ½" from the top and bottom and ⅞" deep.

SERVING TRAY

— 14 —

Cut the splines. With a contrasting piece of wood, cut the splines at the bandsaw. Cut them slightly too thick so you can sand them to a perfect fit.

— 15 —

Sand the splines to fit. Use a sander to thin down the splines until they fit in the grooves.

— 16 —

Shape the splines. Cut out oversized triangles on the bandsaw.

MAKE YOUR OWN KITCHEN TOOLS

SERVING TRAY

— 17 —

Glue in those splines. Leave them oversized and sticking out for now. Let dry.

— 18 —

Cut the splines down to size. Once the glue dries, use a flush-cut trim saw to cut the splines down. If you don't have a flush-cut trim saw, you can also sand them down.

— 19 —

Cut the legs. Cut four 8"-long pieces to ¾" x ¾" to use as legs.

SERVING TRAY

— 20 —

Add a roundover to each. On one end of all four pieces, use a coin to draw a roundover.

— 21 —

Sand down to the line. There's not much material to remove, so this can easily be done with a disc sander or palm sander.

— 22 —

Drill a hole for leg reinforcement. Use a drill press or handheld drill to make a ½"-diameter hole that is ⅜" deep and 2" in from the edge without the roundover. This is going to hold a ½"-diameter dowel for added leg strength.

SERVING TRAY

— 23 —

Measure the dowel. Place your legs inside the glued-up assembly to determine the length of dowel needed. Notice the pencil marks indicating how deep the holes are to help locate the right length for the dowel.

— 24 —

Cut the dowels. Using a bandsaw or hand saw, cut two dowels to length.

SERVING TRAY

— 25 —

Glue together the two leg assemblies. Make sure the dowels are seated with taps from the rubber mallet.

— 26 —

Add bolts for pivoting legs. Use a set of connecting bolts and connecting cap nuts to allow the legs to pivot. If they are a little too long, you can easily cut them to size later.

MAKE YOUR OWN KITCHEN TOOLS

SERVING TRAY

— 27 —

Drill a hole for the bolts. On the rounded-over end of all four legs, drill a hole through for the connecting bolts. The bolts pictured require a ¼"-diameter hole drilled in ½" from the end.

— 28 —

Drill a second hole for the bolts. To connect the leg to the tray, drill a ¼"-diameter hole on the tray assembly 1½" in from the edge and ⅜" from the bottom.

SERVING TRAY

— 29 —
Cut the bolts to size. The connecting bolts are too long so they are cut down to size by removing ½" with a hacksaw.

— 30 —
Assemble the connecting bolts with hex keys. This should allow you to fold and unfold the legs as necessary.

— 31 —
Finish the tray. Finally, apply a final sanding and a finish of your choice.

KITCHEN TOOL
SPOON & SPATULA

You'll flip over this matched utensil set.

TOOLS
- Bandsaw with resawing blade and 3/16" 4 TPI skiptooth blade
- Pencil
- Carving knife
- Deep hook carving knife
- Drill with 1/4" wood bit
- Coping saw
- Chisel
- Rasp
- Food-safe finish

MATERIALS
- Slice of green wood or firewood, about 12" long

Wooden spoons and spatulas are the mainstays of the cooking range. Whether stirring sauce or flipping fish, you can never have too many wooden utensils on hand. Never worry about scraping the finish on a cast-iron or non-stick pan, either. After you make your first pair, you'll be looking for excuses to make more! The best part is customizing the business ends to be as thick or thin as you like.

TEMPLATE

Photocopy these templates at 200%.

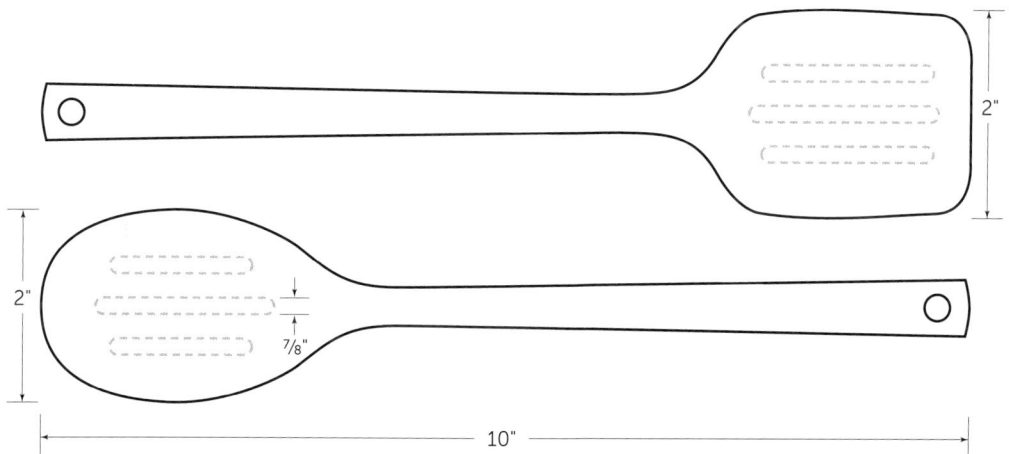

SPOON & SPATULA

— 1 —

For this project, start off with some firewood or green wood. You can use kiln dried wood, but it will be a little harder to hand carve in future steps.

— 2 —

Resaw your log into a 1¼"-thick piece. It helps to have a blade made for resawing large pieces of wood.

— 3 —

Trace an outline onto your board. Templates that have been printed out and cut to size help a lot.

96 MAKE YOUR OWN KITCHEN TOOLS

SPOON & SPATULA

— 4 —

Place a smaller blade on your bandsaw and cut out the outlines. To help turn tight corners, use a 3/16" 4 TPI blade.

— 5 —

Flip the utensils on their sides and draw the profile curves. I'm freehanding and drawing what appears correct. If you're making a spoon, make sure you leave enough thickness at the top to createthe spoon's bowl.

— 6 —

Cut the profile on the bandsaw. Safety warning: Be sure the front and the back of your blank are placed firmly on the bandsaw table. If not, as the piece enters the blade, it may catch and the bandsaw can potentially pull the piece and your hands toward the blade.

MAKE YOUR OWN KITCHEN TOOLS

SPOON & SPATULA

— 7 —

Shape the utensils. Use any method you like to shape them. Sanding, rasps, or files will work. I'm using a carving knife, which slices through green wood with ease.

— 8 —

For the spoon bowl, you can use a deep hook carving knife. I find it very satisfying and rewarding to use. If you're using power tools, a rotary tool with a sphere burr bit will make quick work of this.

SPOON & SPATULA

— 9 —

Draw the slots. To make the slotted spoons and spatulas, draw three parallel lines.

— 10 —

Drill the ends of the slots. At the end of each line, drill a ¼"-diameter hole.

MAKE YOUR OWN KITCHEN TOOLS

SPOON & SPATULA

— 11 —
Use a coping saw to connect the dots. Saw slow and steady with a sharp blade to make nice, clean lines.

— 12 —
Complete the slots. Clean up the cuts with a chisel and a rasp.

SPOON & SPATULA

— 13 —

In the end of the handle, drill a ¼"-diameter hole. Even if you don't plan on hanging the utensils, the hole adds a nice touch.

— 14 —

Apply the finish. Finally, finish off your spoons and spatulas with a food-safe finish or wax.

MAKE YOUR OWN KITCHEN TOOLS 101

KITCHEN TOOL
TRIVET

This snazzy trivet is a hot little number.

TOOLS

- Tablesaw and push stick
- Pencil
- Ruler
- Bandsaw
- Spindle sander
- Drill with 1" Forstner bit
- Wood glue
- Painter's tape
- Router with chamfer or roundover bit
- Random orbital sander with sandpaper up to 220 grit
- Food-safe finish

MATERIALS

- 4 frames, hardwood, ¾" x 1¼" x 7¼"
- Support, plywood, ⅛" x 6⅜" x 6⅜"
- Heatproof surface, 6" tile (actual measurement is 5⅞")

This project was inspired by Grandpa Picciuto, who has made many of these trivets for family and friends. My grandfather is the biggest inspiration in what I do—he still finds time to get into the shop and do woodworking almost every single day. Get inspired and crank out a shopful of your own trivets! Make them as straightforward or complex as you like. You can also size the trivet to your needs by changing the length of the frame sides.

PLAN

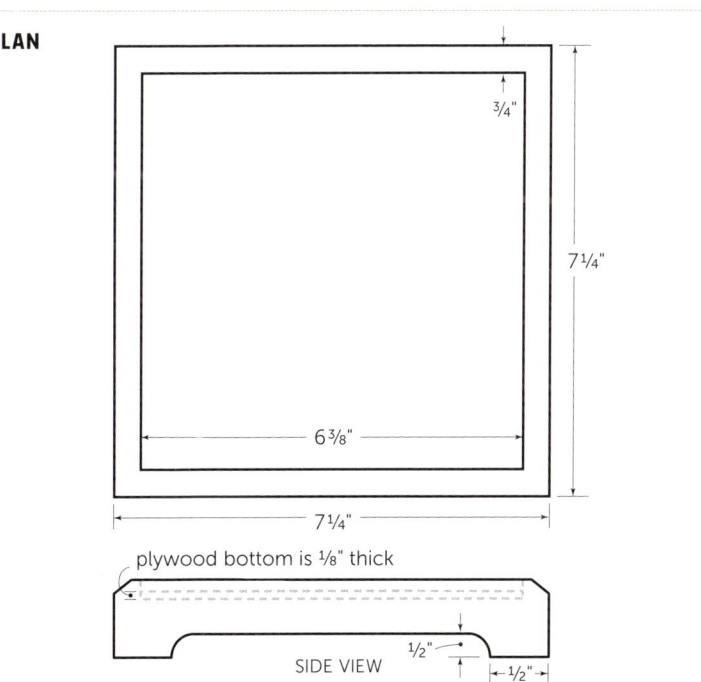

TRIVET

— 1 —

Start with a ¾"-thick, solid piece of wood. The pictured piece will be more than plenty, but at a minimum, you'll need wood that's 16" long and 3" wide.

— 2 —

Start cutting the strips. On the tablesaw, cut two strips measuring 1¼" wide.

— 3 —

Cut the frame. Set your blade to 45° and cut four pieces with the longest edge measuring 7¼" long. We'll call these pieces the frame, since it will hold the plywood bottom like a picture frame.

TRIVET

— 4 —

Cut the groove. Set the tablesaw blade to ¼" high and cut a groove ³⁄₁₆" in on the inside face of all four frame pieces. This groove is going to hold the plywood bottom. Note: If you are using a thin kerf blade, you may need to make two passes to get a ⅛" groove.

— 5 —

Cut a piece of ⅛" plywood to fit in the groove. The final dimensions should be approximately 6⅜" x 6⅜". Check the fit. Slightly too small is ok, but too big and the four frame pieces will not assemble correctly.

— 6 —

Rough assemble the trivet to see if your tile will fit. I've found that tiles can vary in size. As you can see in the photo, my tile is slightly too big and doesn't drop in, so we'll open the frame up slightly in the next step.

MAKE YOUR OWN KITCHEN TOOLS   105

TRIVET

— 7 —

Thin the frame if necessary. Set the blade height to just higher than the groove and move your fence to remove a very small amount of material. Run all four frame pieces through. Check your fit and repeat if necessary, sneaking up on the perfect fit.

— 8 —

Create feet on the corners. Draw a line ½" up from the bottom and 1" from the edge, and round the corner where the lines meet. This material will be removed.

TRIVET

— 9 —

Remove the material. Use the bandsaw to cut just inside the line.

— 10 —

Shape the feet. Sand down to the line with a spindle sander or sanding tools of choice.

— 11 —

Drill a tile-removal hole. Before gluing up the trivet, drill a 1"-diameter hole in the middle of the plywood bottom. This will allow for easy tile removal by pushing through the bottom with your finger.

MAKE YOUR OWN KITCHEN TOOLS

TRIVET

— 12 —
Glue it up. Add wood glue to the mitered corners, as well as the plywood groove, and clamp it all together. On a small project like this, painter's tape makes a great clamp.

— 13 —
Once the glue dries, roundover or chamfer the top edge. This is purely a design choice, but I like how the chamfer lightens up the overall look of the trivet.

TRIVET

— 14 —
Make it smooth. Sand everything up to 220 grit.

— 15 —
To wrap it up, add your favorite finish. Any finish will do because this does not have to be food safe. Drop in your tile and you're good to go.

MAKE YOUR OWN KITCHEN TOOLS 109

KITCHEN TOOL
UTENSIL HOLDER

Round up your cooking utensils in this sleek holder.

Never lose your favorite cooking implements in an inconvenient drawer again! This bold utensil holder is the perfect design to highlight any wood with striking grain. The contrasting accent around the top of the project is the icing on the cake. With how quickly and easily the pieces glue up, soon every homeowner on your gift list will have one on their counter.

TOOLS

> Planer
> Tablesaw with push stick and miter gauge fence
> Wood glue
> Random orbital sander
> Digital angle gauge
> Painter's tape
> Pencil
> Ruler
> Bandsaw
> Drill with ⅜" wood bit
> Cyanoacrylate glue
> Router with 45° chamfer bit
> Finish

MATERIALS

> 10 sides, hardwood, ½" x 1⅝" x 9"
> 10 contrasting stripes, hardwood, ⅛" x ¼" x 1⅝"
> Bottom, plywood, ⅛" x 6" x 6 "

PLAN

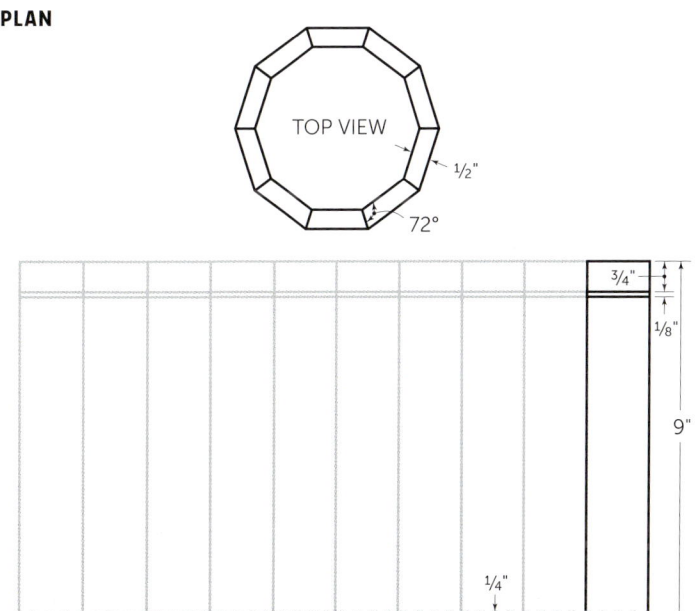

MAKE YOUR OWN KITCHEN TOOLS   111

UTENSIL HOLDER

— 1 —

Plane down your material to ½" thick. I'm starting with a piece of walnut that's 5½" wide by 38" long.

— 2 —

Cut the board. Cross-cut your board into four 9" pieces.

UTENSIL HOLDER

— 3 —

Cut a groove that'll hold the bottom.
Set your tablesaw blade to ¼" high.

— 4 —

With a miter gauge on your tablesaw, set your stop ¼" away from the blade.
Cut a groove into one side of all your pieces. It's important that you use a miter gauge or sled for this cut to avoid dangerous kickback.

— 5 —

Cut an optional decorative element.
Set your stop ¾" away from the blade and cut a groove on the opposite side and face. This space will be filled with contrasting pieces of wood in the next steps.

MAKE YOUR OWN KITCHEN TOOLS

UTENSIL HOLDER

— 6 —

To fill that gap, cut some thin strips of contrasting wood on the tablesaw. This might take a few tries to find the perfect fit. Approximate size will be ⅛" thick and ¼" wide, depending on the width and depth of the groove.

— 7 —

Glue the contrasting piece in place with some wood glue. If the fit is nice and snug, there should be no need for clamps or tape.

UTENSIL HOLDER

— 8 —
Sand the surface. Once the glue dries, sand it smooth and flush with sanding tools of your choice.

— 9 —
Cut the sides. Use the tablesaw to rip 10 pieces to 1⅝" wide.

— 10 —
Cut the angled sides. Set your tablesaw blade to 72° and cut the angled sides. Digital angle gauges are very accurate.

UTENSIL HOLDER

— 11 —

Nudge the fence over and cut one side.
Flip the piece around and cut the other side.
Do not adjust the fence between the cuts.
Repeat this until all 10 pieces have been cut.
BE SURE the outside of the piece—the side
with the contrasting wood—is facing up.

— 12 —

Clamp the sides. With all the pieces cut, line them up with the outside facing up and tape them together. This is how we'll clamp the project when it comes time for the glue-up.

UTENSIL HOLDER

— 13 —
Roughly assemble the container.
Roll the sides together and trace the outside shape, as well as the inside shape, onto a ⅛"-thick piece of plywood.

— 14 —
Draw the shape. From here, draw a ¼" offset from the inside line. That should be equal to the depth of your groove cut in step 4.

MAKE YOUR OWN KITCHEN TOOLS

UTENSIL HOLDER

— 15 —

Cut the bottom. Cut this shape out at the bandsaw and test the fit.

— 16 —

In the middle, drill a ⅜" drainage hole. This is just in case wet utensils get stored in the container so the water can have a place to go.

118   MAKE YOUR OWN KITCHEN TOOLS

UTENSIL HOLDER

— 17 —

Glue everything up. Spread some glue between all the seams and place in your plywood bottom.

— 18 —

No need for clamps. Just tape it up and let it dry for a few hours.

UTENSIL HOLDER

— 19 —

Sand the surface. Sand everything smooth.

— 20 —

Fill any gaps. If you notice any gaps in the seams, they can easily be filled with some cyanoacrylate glue.

UTENSIL HOLDER

— 21 —

Add a decorative chamfer. This is optional; add a 45° chamfer to the top, as well as the bottom. Visually, I prefer a chamfer, but a roundover will do as well.

— 22 —

Finish the project. Apply your favorite food-safe finish.

KITCHEN TOOL
SPICE RACK

Add some zest with this colorful spice rack.

TOOLS

- Tablesaw and push stick
- Wood glue and epoxy
- Clamps
- Drill with ¼" and ⅜" wood bits and ⅞" Forstner bit
- Painter's tape
- Flush-cut trim saw
- Miter saw
- Mallet
- Dowel centers

This nifty design adds acrylic sheets into the mix for a pop of color. Match the shades to your kitchen for a rack that blends into the decor, or select contrasting hues to make a spicy statement. With a little tweaking, you can expand or contract the dimensions of this rack to house both the quantity and container size of the flavorful seasonings your family prefers. Adjust the height to your liking—just be sure to attach the top to the wall with a screw so the rack doesn't tip over.

MATERIALS

- 2 long frames, hardwood, ¾" x 2" x 24½"
- 2 short frames, hardwood, ¾" x 2" x 11"
- 2 dividers, hardwood, ¾" x 1¾" x 11"
- 8 frame dowels, ¼" dia. x 1"
- 2 long face frames, hardwood, ¾" x ¾" x 24½"
- 2 short face frames, hardwood, ¾" x ¾" x 11¾"
- 2 doors, acrylic, ⅛" x 9¼" x 11"
- 2 feet, hardwood, ¾" x 1¾" x 2¾"
- 4 feet dowels, ⅜" dia. x 1"
- 12 spacers, hardwood, ¼" x 2⁷⁄₁₆" x 2⅞"
- 4 oversized spacers, hardwood, ¼" x 2¾" x 2⅞"
- 2 shelves, acrylic, ⅛" x 2" x 9"
- 1 back, acrylic, ⅛" x 11" x 24½

MAKE YOUR OWN KITCHEN TOOLS

SPICE RACK

PLAN

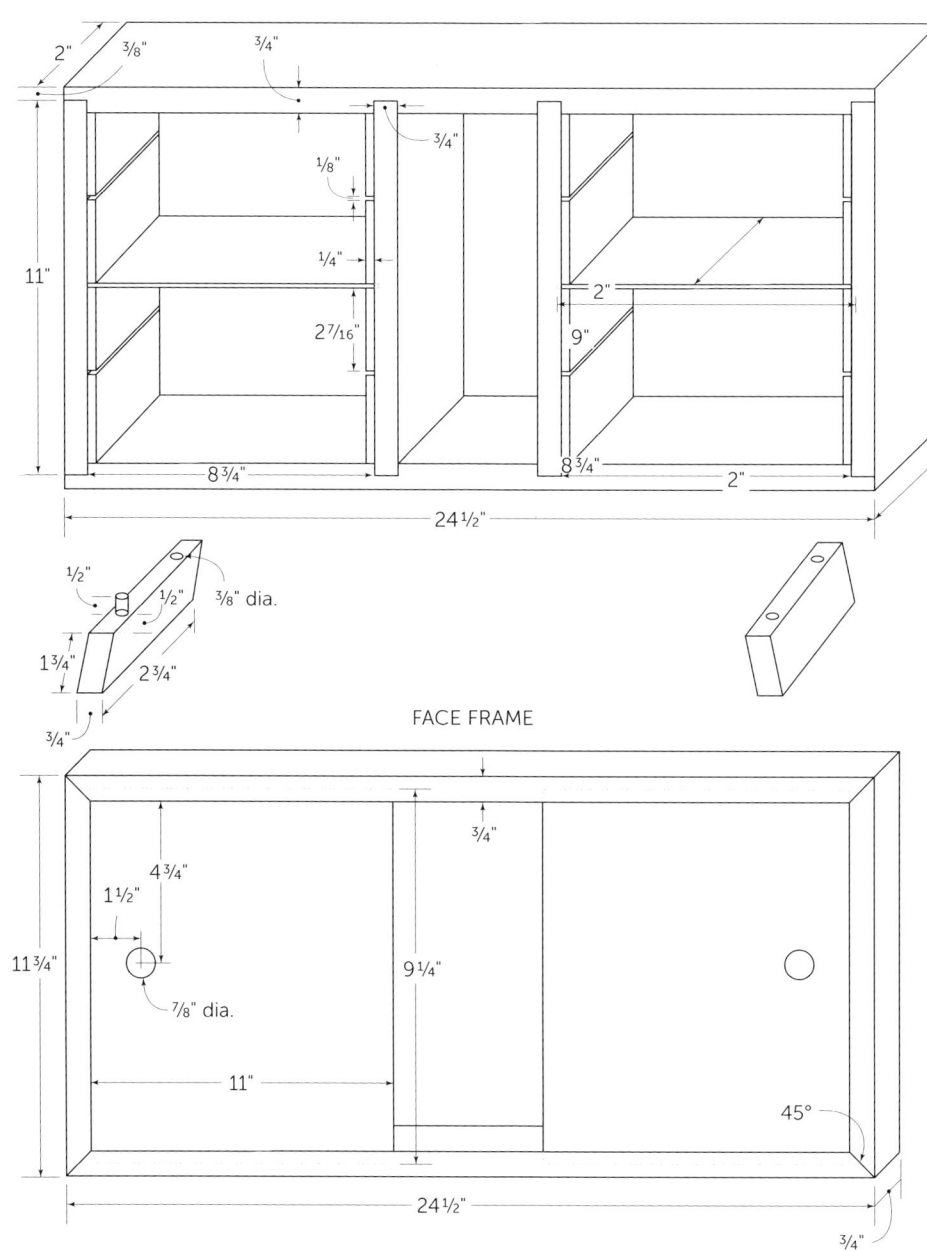

FACE FRAME

SPICE RACK

— 1 —

Rip some ¾" hardwood to 2" wide. We'll need two pieces that are 24½" long and two pieces that are 11" long.

— 2 —

Rabbet the long frame pieces. On both ends of the two 24½" pieces, cut a rabbet ½" deep and ¾" wide.

MAKE YOUR OWN KITCHEN TOOLS 125

SPICE RACK

— 3 —

Cut interior rabbets. Measure in 8¾" from each edge and cut two more rabbets ½" deep and ¾" wide.

— 4 —

The two long pieces should look like this. The distance between the two inside rabbets should measure 5½".

SPICE RACK

— 5 —

Cut the back panel rabbet. Set your blade ½" high and cut a ⅛" rabbet on one side of all four pieces. This rabbet will allow the back panel to be glued on in a later step.

— 6 —

Cut the interior dividers. Saw two pieces that are 11" long, 1¾" wide, and ¾" thick. They will fit in the interior dadoes cut earlier.

SPICE RACK

— 7 —

Assemble the frame. You can now assemble and glue the six pieces you've cut.

— 8 —

Prepare to add dowels. Once the glue dries, drill two ¼" holes 1" deep. Spacing isn't critical, but as shown, the holes are ½" in from the edges.

SPICE RACK

— 9 —

Add the dowels. Apply some glue, pound in a ¼" dowel, and use a flush-cut trim saw to cut off the excess. Do this with all four corner joints.

— 10 —

Rip the face frame wood. These will hold the sliding door panels. You'll need about 7' of ¾" x ¾". No need to cut to exact length yet, but the final length will be two pieces at 24½" long and two pieces at 11¾" long.

MAKE YOUR OWN KITCHEN TOOLS

SPICE RACK

— 11 —

Cut a rabbet and dado. These face frame pieces are going to hold the sliding doors. Set your tablesaw blade to ½" high. Cut a ⅛"-wide rabbet on one edge and a ⅛"-wide dado ¼" in from the other side, as seen in this photo.

— 12 —

Cut the 45° miters. Cut the face frames double-stacked at the miter saw so each pair will be the exact same length. You'll want two pieces 24½" long and two pieces 11¾" long.

— 13 —

Cut the two sliding doors. For this project, I'm using ⅛" red acrylic. You can also use ⅛" plywood and stain or paint it. Cut two pieces 9¼" wide and 11" tall.

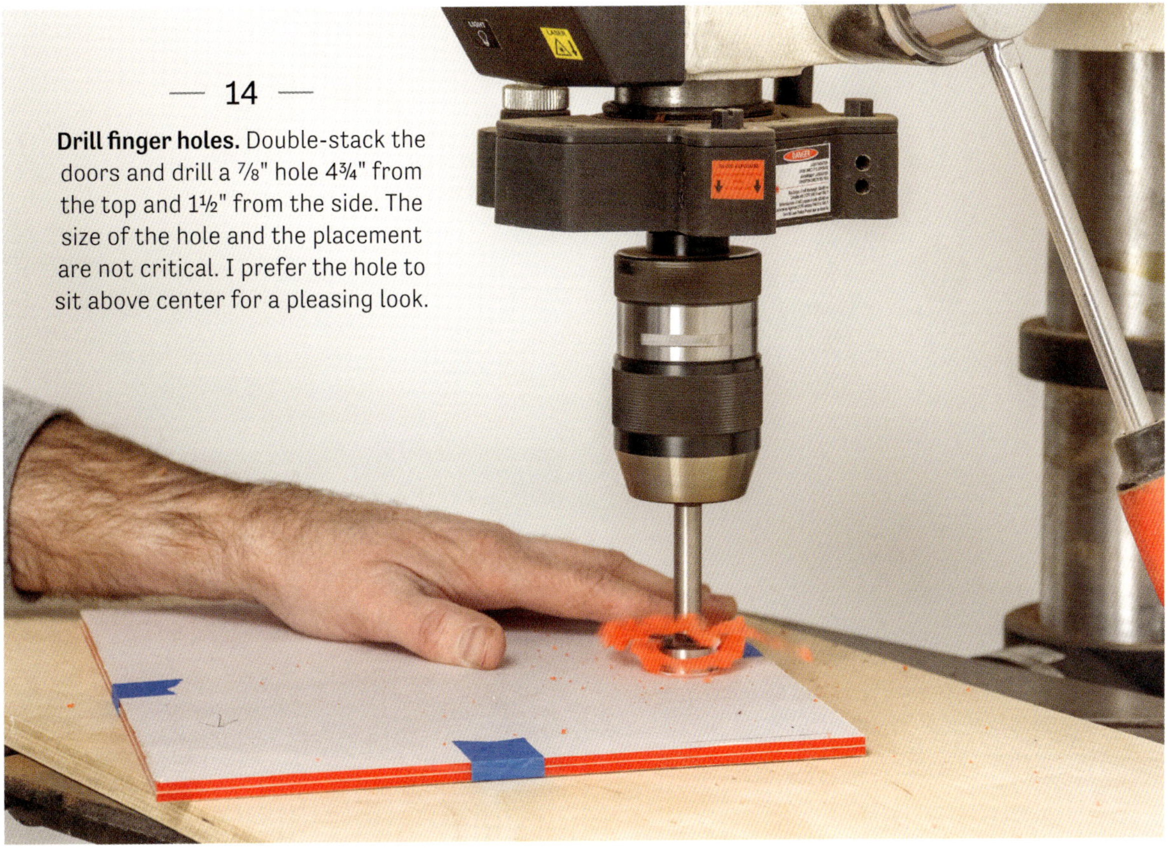

SPICE RACK

— 14 —

Drill finger holes. Double-stack the doors and drill a 7/8" hole 4¾" from the top and 1½" from the side. The size of the hole and the placement are not critical. I prefer the hole to sit above center for a pleasing look.

— 15 —

Glue up the face frame. Place one sliding door into the dado and glue the four mitered corners together like a picture frame. If you have a band clamp, use that. Otherwise, painter's tape works well.

MAKE YOUR OWN KITCHEN TOOLS

SPICE RACK

— 16 —

When the face frame is dry, glue to the assembly. Use wood glue and clamps to secure everything. Be sure to place in your second sliding door between the face frame and the back frame before gluing.

— 17 —

Make the feet. Set your blade to 75° and cut two pieces 1¾" long. This length can be any size, depending on how high you'd like the spice rack to set above the counter. The width of these pieces should be 2¾".

— 18 —

Prepare to attach the feet to the assembly. We're going to use ⅜" dowels. On the top of each foot, drill two evenly spaced ⅜" holes ½" deep.

SPICE RACK

— 19 —

Insert two ⅜" dowel centers into the holes as seen here. These will help align the holes on the bottom of the spice rack.

— 20 —

Place the foot where you'd like to attach it and give it a light tap with a mallet. This will leave indentations in the assembly, letting you know where to drill the holes.

— 21 —

Drill the dowel holes. Use the ⅜" drill bit to make two holes centered on the indentations and ½" deep.

SPICE RACK

— 22 —

Attach the dowels. Cut 3/8" dowels to just less than 1" in length, remove the dowel centers, and glue the foot in place. Repeat on the other side with the other foot.

— 23 —

Cut the spacers for the adjustable shelves. The exact measurements of the 1/4"-thick spacers can be tricky, so cut 12 pieces to exact size (2 7/8" wide by 2 7/16" long) and four pieces oversized (2 7/8" wide by 2 3/4" long) so they can be trimmed to fit.

— 24 —

Glue in the spacers. Start from the bottom and glue in the first three pieces. Use your 1/8" plywood or acrylic to set a gap between each spacer. For the final spacer, you'll need to trim the oversized piece to fit.

SPICE RACK

— 25 —

Finally, cut the acrylic for the shelves and back. The exact size may vary, so cut the shelves and back panel to fit.

— 26 —

Glue on the back. I did not have an acrylic sheet large enough, so I pieced together three pieces. This isn't a problem because the seams will be hidden by the two dividers. Set the shelf on your counter or use screws to mount it to the wall.

KITCHEN TOOL
PIZZA PEEL

A handmade peel for a handmade pie.

TOOLS

- Planer
- Miter saw
- Wood glue
- Clamps
- Pencil
- Large compass or pizza pan, and spray paint can, to trace curves
- Ruler
- Bandsaw
- Disc sander
- Spindle sander
- Rotary tool
- Belt sander
- Router with ¾" roundover bit
- Drill with 1" Forstner bit
- Random orbital sander with sandpaper up to 220 grit
- Food-safe finish

MATERIALS

- 2 outsides, hardwood, ½" x 5½" x 15"
- Center, hardwood, ½" x 3¾" x 30"
- Handle, hardwood, ¾" x 3¾" x 15"

Homemade pizza is a mainstay at my house, but I never knew how much I needed a pizza peel until I made one. It's great for getting pies in and out of the oven and comes in handy for slicing and serving as well. When not in use, it's as handsome hanging on your kitchen wall as it is useful on pizza night.

PLAN

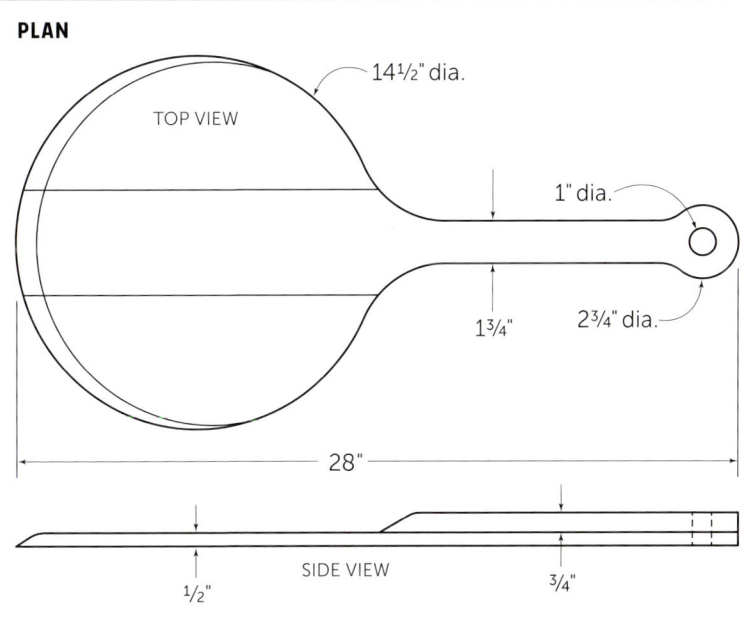

MAKE YOUR OWN KITCHEN TOOLS 137

PIZZA PEEL

— 1 —
Buy or plane your stock. You can plane thicker stock down to ½", or buy pre-thickenessed ½"-thick stock from your local hardwood dealer.

— 2 —
Survey your stock. The combination of mahogany and hickory lend a nice look to this design, but any contrasting, food-safe hardwoods would work as well.

— 3 —
Rough out the stock. Begin by crosscutting the two outside pieces (hickory) to roughly 15" long and the single middle piece (mahogany) to roughly 30".

PIZZA PEEL

— 4 —

Glue it up. Clamp and glue everything together, trying to keep all the pieces level and aligned. Spring clamps positioned at the joint lines help keep the pieces aligned.

— 5 —

Draw out a circle. You can use a large compass or outline the profile of a round pan. Shown here is a 14½" pizza pan.

MAKE YOUR OWN KITCHEN TOOLS 139

PIZZA PEEL

— 6 —

Draw out the handle. The straight portion of the handle is 1¾" wide. To create the curved transition from the handle to the rounded portion of the board, you can draw the curve freehand or trace the pattern off a can, jar, or large washer.

— 7 —

Round the end. At the end of the handle, draw out another circle—tracing the base of a spray paint can works perfectly. Again, blend the transition from the circle into the handle lines. The total length of the pizza peel should be about 28".

PIZZA PEEL

— 8 —

Cut the peel to shape. Cut out the shape of the peel at the bandsaw. Trim as close to the line as possible, making sure you don't actually cut into or over the line. In later steps you can refine and finalize the shape.

— 9 —

Clean up the edges. Use a disc sander to sand down to the layout lines on the convex edges of the peel.

— 10 —

Smooth the handle. A spindle sander does a good job of fairing and smoothing the tight inside corners on the handle.

MAKE YOUR OWN KITCHEN TOOLS

PIZZA PEEL

— 11 —

Build up the handle. To make the handle a little more comfortable to use, thicken it up by adding another piece of mahogany. Trace the handle profile onto a piece of ¾" mahogany.

— 12 —

Cut to the line. Cut out the handle shape at the bandsaw. Again, cut as close as possible to the line without touching it.

PIZZA PEEL

— 13 —

Create a transition.
Where the handle meets the large round end of the peel, draw a curve that will blend into the main part of the pizza peel.

— 14 —

Cut out the waste. Back at the bandsaw, cut to the line to remove the waste from the transition area on the handle addition.

MAKE YOUR OWN KITCHEN TOOLS

PIZZA PEEL

— 15 —

Cut a smooth transition. Create a bevel onto the additional handle stock so that it will blend into the large end of the peel. A rotary tool works well to remove the wood, but a rasp and file would work as well.

— 16 —

Clamp it up. Glue and clamp the new handle material to the main handle of the peel.

— 17 —

Smooth it out. Once the glue dries, sand everything flush at the spindle sander or with a file and sandpaper.

PIZZA PEEL

— 18 —

Draw out the bevel. A bevel on the front edge of a peel allows it to slide under a pizza easily. You can draw out the guidelines for the bevel freehand. Draw the line in from the edge about 1" at the end and taper it down so that it's flush at the sides of the peel.

— 19 —

Shape the bevel. File or sand away the wood to create a nice wedge shape on the front of the peel. This can be done quickly with a belt sander and 80-grit sandpaper.

MAKE YOUR OWN KITCHEN TOOLS 145

PIZZA PEEL

— 20 —

Round the handle edges. Use a ¾" roundover bit in your router table to soften the edges of the handle. You only need to round over the top face of the handle. The bottom of the handle and the pizza area will have a much smaller roundover, which can be shaped by hand.

— 21 —

Drill it out. Centered on the round end of the handle, drill a 1" hole so you can hang up your peel for storage and display.

— 22 —

Sand it smooth. Sand the faces up to 220 grit using a random orbit sander. Be sure to blend all the curves and round over any sharp edges.

PIZZA PEEL

— 23 —
Finish it off. This board was finished using a heavy coat of food-grade mineral oil and paraffin wax, but any food-safe finish would work.

— 24 —
Have a slice! All that's left to do is bake a pizza and put your pizza peel to use.

MAKE YOUR OWN KITCHEN TOOLS   147

KITCHEN TOOL
TABLET HOLDER

An elegant piece to prop up your recipe.

TOOLS

- Clamps
- Bandsaw
- Spindle sander
- Belt sander
- Packing tape
- Spray adhesive
- Wood glue
- Router with ½" roundover bit
- Tablesaw with push stick
- Finish with brush

MATERIALS

- Foam sheet
- Press, inexpensive wood, 2" x 6" x 36", glued up to 4 ½" x 5" x 11"
- Holder, (6) paper-backed veneer sheets, 5½" x 16"
- Lip, hardwood, 4½" x ¾" x ½"

This curvaceous project is a great introduction to both veneering and woodbending. With minimal material and time invested, you can get a taste for whether you enjoy those techniques. Use the finished holder to prop up your tablet or a recipe card while cooking.

TEMPLATE

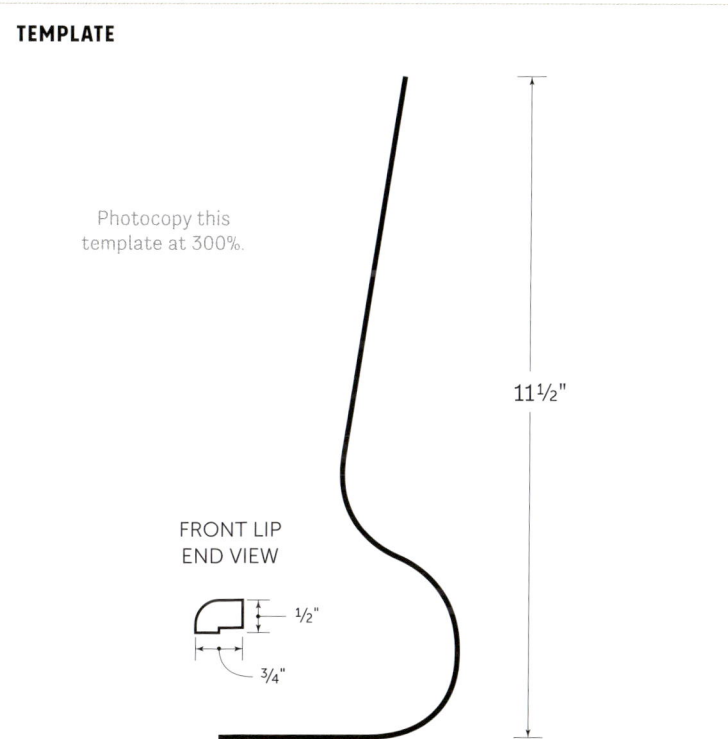

Photocopy this template at 300%.

11½"

FRONT LIP END VIEW

½"

¾"

MAKE YOUR OWN KITCHEN TOOLS

TABLET HOLDER

— 1 —

Glue up a block of wood for the form. This can be any cheap inexpensive wood. I'm using a 2x6 from the home center. The final size of the block after glue up is 4½" x 5" x 11".

— 2 —

Attach the template. Copy the template on page 149. Attach it to the side of the blank with spray adhesive.

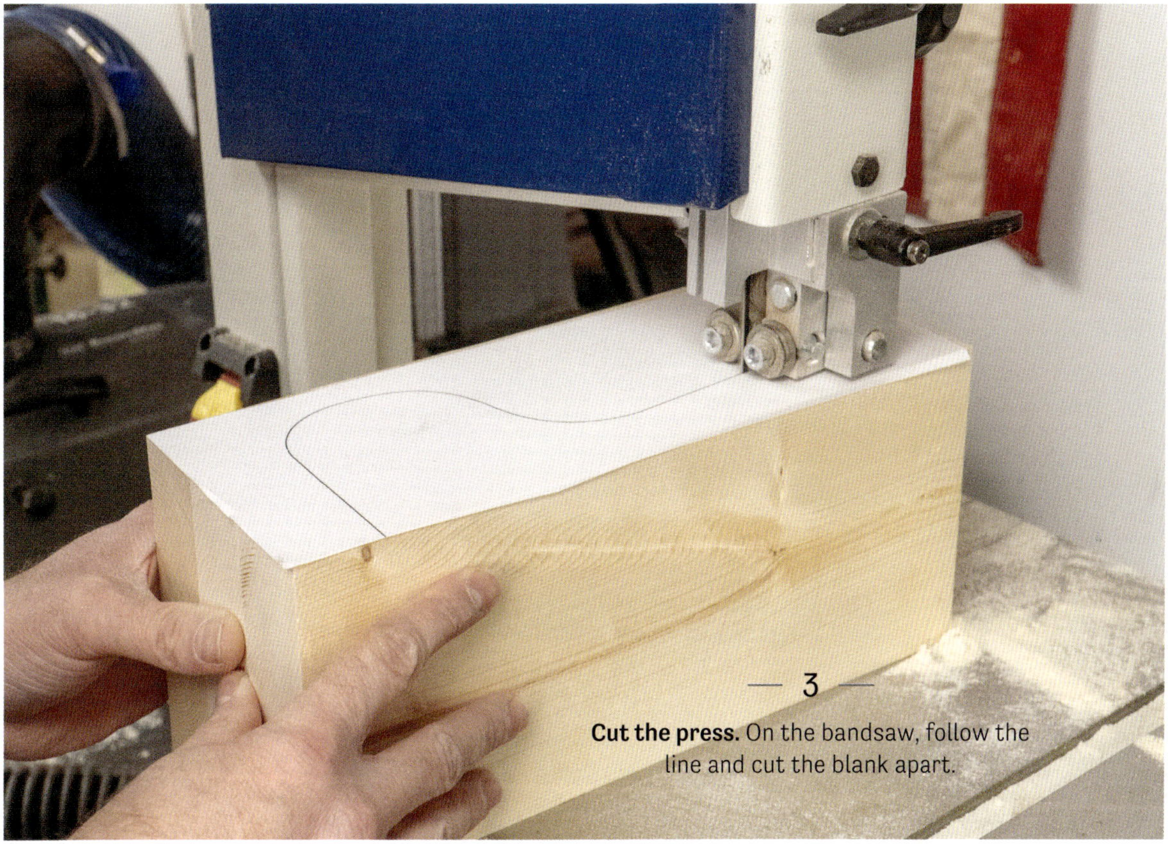

TABLET HOLDER

— 3 —
Cut the press. On the bandsaw, follow the line and cut the blank apart.

— 4 —
Sand it down. Remove another 1/16" of material on both sides. This will ensure that the liner and veneers fit in properly.

TABLET HOLDER

— 5 —

Line the press. To help put pressure on all parts of the veneer, I line the inside of both pieces with foam sheets you can find at any craft store. The sheets have a bit of squishiness, allowing pressure at all angles. Cover the entire surface with packing tape. Glue does not adhere, so any squeeze-out will not glue your form together.

— 6 —

Cut the veneer. Cut six sheets to 16" long and 5½" wide. These will be slightly oversized and stick out the form. The veneer I'm using is paper backed, which allows it to bend more without cracking and works great for this type of project.

TABLET HOLDER

— 7 —

Apply the glue. Spread plenty of glue on what will be the inside layers of the lamination. Make sure a wood side is showing on the veneers facing out on both the top and bottom of the stack.

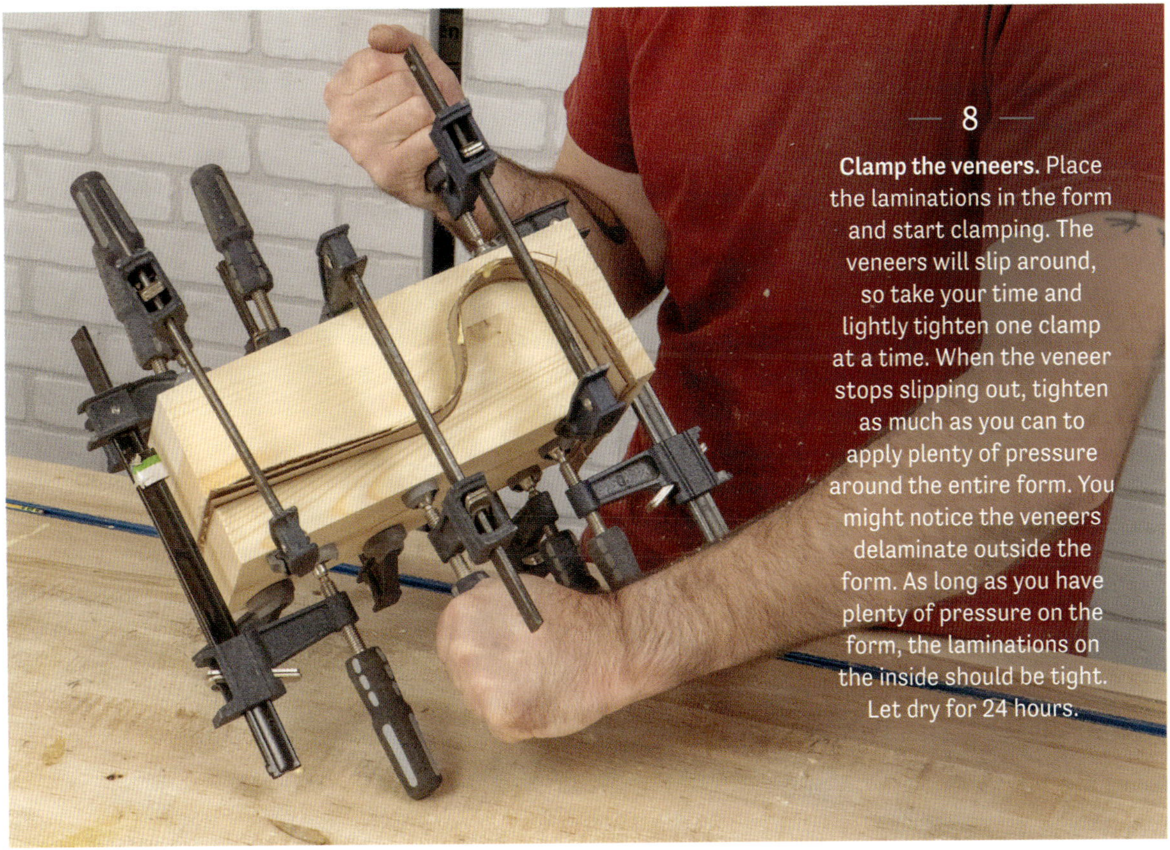

— 8 —

Clamp the veneers. Place the laminations in the form and start clamping. The veneers will slip around, so take your time and lightly tighten one clamp at a time. When the veneer stops slipping out, tighten as much as you can to apply plenty of pressure around the entire form. You might notice the veneers delaminate outside the form. As long as you have plenty of pressure on the form, the laminations on the inside should be tight. Let dry for 24 hours.

MAKE YOUR OWN KITCHEN TOOLS

TABLET HOLDER

— 9 —

Cut to rough shape. Once dry, pull the piece out of the form and cut off the edges at the bandsaw. Make sure the piece is always stable so the blade doesn't grab the piece out of your hand. The final width should be 4½", but it's not critical to be exact.

— 10 —

Sand the edges. Smooth it out with a final sanding on the edges using a belt or random orbit sander.

TABLET HOLDER

— 11 —

Draw the corners. For a more decorative look, use a spray paint can or a similarly curved item and draw rounded corners.

— 12 —

Cut the corners. Cut off the rounded corners with a bandsaw.

TABLET HOLDER

— 13 —

Round the front lip. You'll need a piece that's 4½" long and ¾" thick. The width doesn't matter at this point, but make it wide enough to work easily on the tablesaw. Round over one of the longer sides with a ½" roundover bit.

— 14 —

Cut off the piece. Cut off ½" of the rounded end with the tablesaw. Rounding over and then cutting is much safer than working with a small piece at the router table.

— 15 —

Cut a rabbet. Set the tablesaw blade height to the thickness of your tablet holder, which should be around ⅛". Nibble away a rabbet that'll be glued to the laminated piece, as seen in step 17.

TABLET HOLDER

— 16 —

Dry-fit the lip. Check the front lip until you get the perfect fit. Glue it on.

— 17 —

Clamp the lip. To hold the front lip in place while the glue dries, spring clamps or painter's tape should provide plenty of strength.

— 18 —

Apply finish. And, finally, give the stand some coats of your favorite finish to make it shine.

CHOOSING & USING FOOD-SAFE FINISHES

There are many ways to finish wooden kitchen utensils and no finish is maintenance free. The more you use the utensils, the more you'll need to apply additional finish. The finish I like to use takes a two-step process. The first step is applying mineral oil that seeps deep into the wood, and the second step adds a protective film on top of the surface.

Lumber Choice Comes First

In general, when choosing woods for utensils, look for dense hardwoods, as they are more durable and can stand up to kitchen tasks. You should also lean toward woods that don't contain an excess of natural oils. Some people have a sensitivity to these oils, and you don't want your tools to alter the taste of your food.

Most people also stay away from spalted and reclaimed woods because you don't always know what you're dealing with. If you do use spalted or reclaimed woods, be sure to seal the surface so that it won't affect the food in any way.

In general, North American hardwoods like maple, walnut, and cherry are commonly used in kitchen utensils, and rare exotic woods should be avoided. Whatever woods you choose, do your research on food safety before venturing into the unknown.

1

CHOOSING & USING FOOD-SAFE FINISHES

1 Start with smooth stock. Sand everything down to 220 grit. A good sanding job pays off well on small jobs that beg to be touched.

2 Raise the grain. Use a wet paper towel to raise the grain. The moisture causes some of the wood fibers to swell.

3 Remove the raised grain. Go back and sand everything smooth again with 220-grit sandpaper. This second sanding won't take long to smooth everything back out. This step will keep the utensil smooth after use and washing.

4 Lay on the oil. Coat the entire piece with a heavy dose of white, food-grade mineral oil.

CHOOSING & USING FOOD-SAFE FINISHES

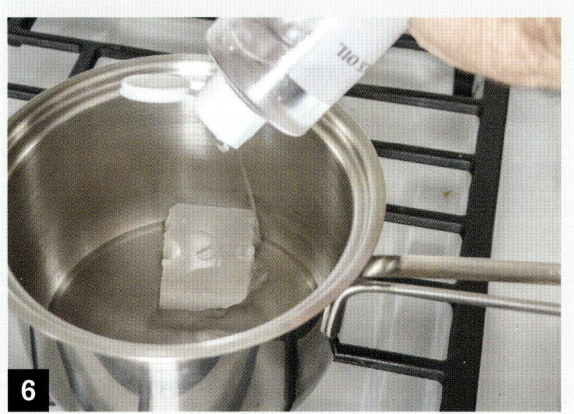

160   MAKE YOUR OWN KITCHEN TOOLS

CHOOSING & USING FOOD-SAFE FINISHES

5 And again . . . Some woods and all end grain soak up a lot of mineral oil. Keep applying more and more until the oil sits on the surface. Allow the oil to sit for a couple of hours before wiping away any excess.

6 Add a little wax. For the second coat, melt paraffin wax on the stove using the lowest heat setting. As the wax melts add a bit of the white, food-grade mineral oil. You'll want about a 50/50 mix.

7 Finish while it's hot. While the wax mixture is still warm, apply a heavy coat to the utensil. Let the wax set for a couple of hours. This will leave a film on the surface but it's easily removed later.

8 Buff it out. Use a soft cloth to buff away the wax. This coat gives your project a protective finish and a satin sheen.

TOOLS YOU WILL NEED

As any woodworker knows, there is more than one way to accomplish most crafting goals. For example, you can drill a hole with a drill press, a handheld electric drill, or even an eggbeater (manual) drill. You might have a high-tech woodshop already set up; or you might only have some basic hand tools. You don't need to run out and buy every tool in existence to create the projects in this book. Below is a list of the types of tools you will need.

Safety equipment
- Dust mask
- Eye protection
- Gloves
- Dust extraction system
- Sacrificial board

Marking and measuring tools
- Pencil
- Permanent marker
- Ruler
- Square
- Sliding T-bevel
- Compass or round items (such as coins and spray paint cans) for tracing circular shapes

Clamps
- Band clamp
- Bar clamps
- F-style clamps
- Spring clamps
- Painter's or masking tape

Carving tools of choice, hand or power
- Hammer or mallet

Drilling equipment
- Drill press
- Handheld drill
- Variety of wood, Forstner, and screwdriver bits

Sawing equipment for straight cuts
- Tablesaw with push stick
- Miter saw or miter gauge fence for tablesaw
- Circular saw
- Flush-cut trim saw
- Hacksaw
- Handsaw

Sawing equipment for freeform cuts
- Bandsaw
- Jigsaw
- Coping saw

Router or router table with a variety of roundover and chamfer bits

Sanding equipment for flattening
- Belt sander
- Random orbital sander
- Disc sander
- Hand plane
- Rasp and file
- Steel wool, #00 to 0000
- 80- to 220-grit sandpaper for method of choice

Sanding equipment for rounding
- Spindle sander
- Drill press with sanding drum
- Round file

Finishes and fasteners
- Food-safe wax, mineral oil, or cutting board finish
- Wood glue
- Epoxy
- Cyanoacrylate glue
- Toothpicks or other disposable glue applicators

METRIC CONVERSIONS

In this book, lengths are given in inches and feet. If you want to convert those to metric measurements, please use the following formulas:

Fractions to Decimals

1/8 = .125
1/4 = .25
1/2 = .5
5/8 = .625
3/4 = .75

Imperial to Metric Conversion

Multiply inches by 25.4 to get millimeters
Multiply inches by 2.54 to get centimeters
Multiply inches by .0254 to get meters

For example, if you wanted to convert 1 1/8 inches to millimeters:
1.125 in. x 25.4mm = 28.575mm

And to convert 60 inches to meters:
60 in. x .0254m = 1.524m

INDEX

acrylic, working with, 130–132, 135

bark, removing, 48
Beer Caddy, 20–27
bowl, 46–53, 66–77
bowl carving, 49–52
Bread Slicer, 36–45

caddy, 20–27
carving, 49–52, 98
  bowl, 49–52
  power, 50, 51, 98
  spoon bowl, 98
contrasting woods, 57

dividers, making, 125–128
dowel centers, 133
dowels for reinforcing, 26, 89, 129

Egg Tray, 54–59

filling a gap, 35
finishes, food-safe, 158–161
food-safe finishes, 158–161

gaps, filling, 35
gluing up a block, 30, 150
green wood. *See* log.
grooves, cutting, 24, 82, 86, 100, 105, 113

hardwood, about, 9, 158

inlay, creating, 113–115
iPad holder. *See Tablet Holder*.

joints, strengthening, 26

Knife Handle, 60–65
knife kits, working with, 61–65

log, working with a, 48–53, 96–97

metric conversion chart, 163

painter's tape as a clamp, 71, 108, 119
Pizza Peel, 136–147
Pizza Rocker, 8–19
power carving, 50, 51

Rustic Bowl, 46–53

sacrificial board, 57, 64
scales, knife. *See Knife Handle*.
Scoop, 28–35
Segmented Bowl, 66–77
segmented turning, 66–77
Serving Tray, 78–93
shelf, 122–135
slots, creating, 43–44
spacers for shelves, 134
spatula. *See Spoon & Spatula*.
Spice Rack, 122–135
splines, cutting, 86–88
Spoon & Spatula, 94–101
spoon, 94–101
spoon bowl, carving, 98
stainless steel, working with, 10–12

Tablet Holder, 148–157
taper, drawing a, 23
tools you will need, 162
tray, 78–93
Trivet, 102–109
turning, segmented, 66–77

Utensil Holder, 110–121

veneering, 148–157

woodbending, 148–157
woodturning, 73–76

ABOUT THE AUTHOR

Believe it or not, I wasn't born with sawdust in my blood. Over the years, I've pursued a wide range of passions—music, photography, video, web development, graphic design, and now woodworking. While that might seem like a crazy path, I've come to realize they're more similar than you think. They're all creative pursuits, and when you're done, you've made something that wasn't there before. That's kind of amazing, and it's something I think everyone should have the opportunity to experience.

What led me to woodworking? Photography, actually. I was planning to exhibit some of my photos, and I decided to have them framed. That's when I realized how crazy-expensive framing is, so I decided to put my high school woodshop skills to work and build my own. The result was less than ideal, but it got me thinking. Now, Make Something lets me bring all my previous passions together—I get to design the projects, create the music, edit the video, and whatever else.

The thing about creativity is that it starts with your individual imagination. When I produce a video for YouTube, my goal is not necessarily to give you a recipe that you follow to the letter and build an exact replica (although if you want to, knock yourself out). My goal is to inspire your own natural creativity—to think about how the ideas I present can fit with your space and your style. And above all, I hope you're inspired to Make Something.

Also by DAVID PICCIUTO & CEDAR LANE PRESS

The New Bandsaw Book
Techniques and Patterns for the Modern Woodworker

By David Picciuto

$19.95 | 120 Pages

Requiring little material and offering lots of creative fun, the wooden box is a popular project for beginners and advanced craftsman alike. As a huge fan of making boxes, David Picciuto presents his favorites for crafting on your trusty bandsaw. Every project follows a clean step-by-step format with the photos and know-how to make the build easy—and concludes with a "Raise a Glass" sidebar to celebrate your completed box.

Make Your Own Cutting Boards
Smart Projects and Stylish Designs for a Hands-On Kitchen

By David Picciuto

$24.95 | 168 Pages

Cutting boards are the perfect first project or an ideal way to showcase a piece of treasured wood. In *Make Your Own Cutting Boards*, the projects range from simple to complex with designs to suit any style or taste. Best of all, each project can be proudly used every day. Extensive photos and instructions make even the most complex techniques easy to achieve and a gallery of inspiring designs will spark your cutting board creativity.

CEDAR LANE PRESS

Look for these titles wherever books are sold or visit www.cedarlanepress.com.

MORE GREAT BOOKS from
CEDAR LANE PRESS

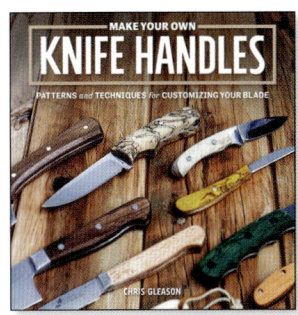

Make Your Own Knife Handles
$24.95 | 168 Pages

The Handmade Skateboard
$24.95 | 160 Pages

Practical Shop Math, 2nd edition
$24.95 | 192 Pages

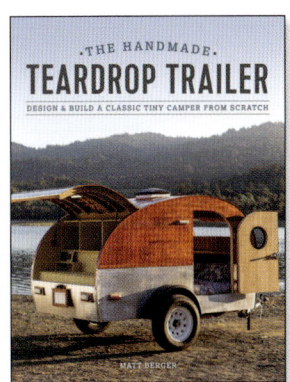

The Handmade Teardrop Trailer
$27.00 | 224 Pages

The Reclaimed Woodworker
$24.95 | 160 Pages

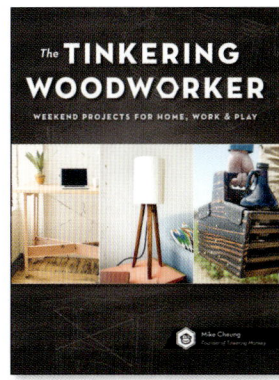

The Tinkering Woodworker
$24.95 | 152 Pages

CEDAR LANE PRESS

Look for these titles wherever books are sold or visit www.cedarlanepress.com.

MORE GREAT BOOKS from
CEDAR LANE PRESS

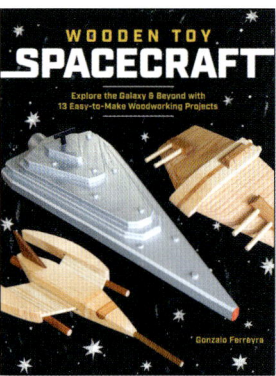

Wooden Toy Spacecraft
$24.95 | 168 Pages

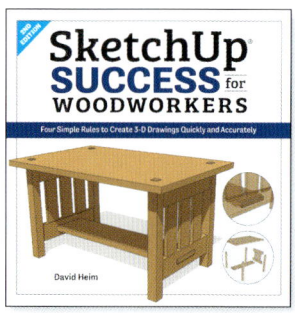

**SketchUp Success
for Woodworkers, 2nd edition**
$24.95 | 120 Pages

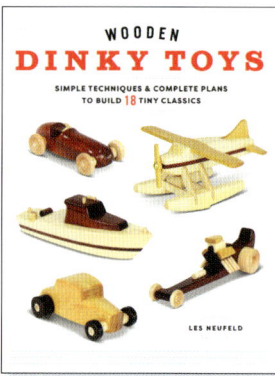

Wooden Dinky Toys
$24.95 | 176 Pages

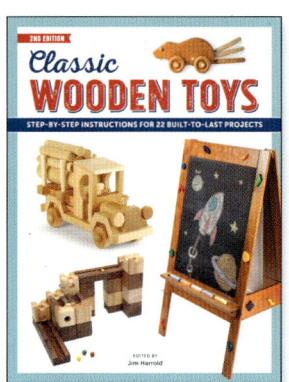

Classic Wooden Toys, 2nd edition
$24.95 | 198 Pages

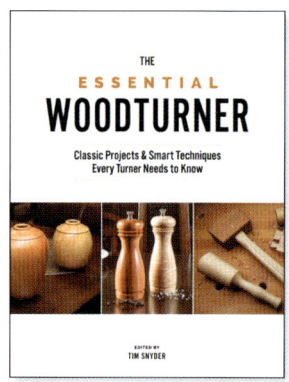

The Essential Woodturner
$27.95 | 228 Pages

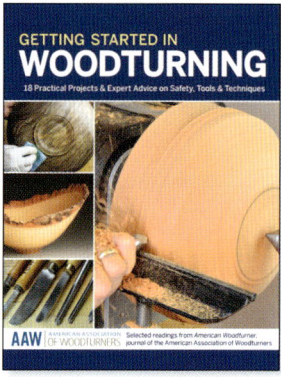

Getting Started in Woodturning
$27.95 | 224 Pages

CEDAR LANE PRESS

Look for these titles wherever books are sold or visit www.cedarlanepress.com.